Mansfield Park

A dramatization by Willis Hall
from the novel by Jane Austen

Samuel French — London
New York - Toronto - Hollywood

MANSFIELD PARK

First presented at the Crucible Theatre, Sheffield, on 4th November, 1993 with the following cast of characters:

Maria Bertram	Tilly Blackwood
Dr Grant/Carpenter	Robin Bowerman
Mrs Grant	Gillian Cally
William Price	Matthew Delamere
Henry Crawford	Peter Hamilton Dyer
Mary Crawford	Amanda Elwes
Gipton	Susan Gardner
Sir Thomas Bertram	Christopher Good
Julia Bertram	Nina Jacques
Edmund Bertram	Mark Jax
Harkness	Clive Kneller
Lady Bertram	Ciaran Madden
Yates	James Mansfield
Reverend Norris	Gordon Langford Rowe
Tom Bertram	Ashley Russell
Fanny Price	Lucy Scott
Mrs Norris	Ursula Smith
Mr Rushworth	Jay Villiers
Braithwaite	Louise Yates

Director	Michael Rudman
Designer	Johan Engels
Musical Director/Arranger	Ewan Anderson
Choreographer	Geraldine Anderson
Sound Designer	Huw Williams
Assistant Director	Zachary Holton
Casting	Wendy Spon
Casting Consultant	Joyce Nettles

Stage Manager	Jerry Knight-Smith
Deputy Stage Manager	Sarah Kingswell
Assistant Stage Manager	Meryl Couper

Stage Management Student on placement from RADA	Harriet Teale

CHARACTERS

Sir Thomas Bertram, of Mansfield Park
Lady Bertram, who married well
Tom Bertram
Edmund Bertram
Maria Bertram
Julia Bertram
Fanny Price, the Bertrams' niece
Mrs Norris, Lady Bertram's parsimonious sister
The Reverend Mr Norris, a clergyman of no great fortune
The Reverend Dr Grant, a clergyman both respectable and
    agreeable
Mrs Grant, who is fifteen years younger than her husband
Henry Crawford, Mrs Grant's step-brother
Mary Crawford, Mrs Grant's step-sister
Mr Rushworth, a gentleman of property and substance
Midshipman William Price, Fanny's sea-going brother
Mr Yates, Tom Bertram's fashionable friend
Harkness
Gipton   } Servants and Narrators
Braithwaite
A Carpenter

SYNOPSIS OF SCENES

AUTHOR'S NOTE

In Michael Rudman's highly-acclaimed original production, at the Crucible Theatre, Sheffield, dance played an integral part: both Acts were preceded by country dances which were performed by the entire company and, similarly, at the final curtain. Although these are not included in this published version, there are two ballroom scenes requiring dancing with the music contained in these pages. But societies whose resources and/or rehearsal schedules preclude the added complication of choreography should not be dissuaded from staging this version of Miss Austen's *Mansfield Park*.

In the first ballroom scene, for example, the action could equally well take place inside the drawing-room, which is being used as an ante-room, with the music drifting in from the ballroom which is out of sight, but close at hand. The actors then would play the dialogue as written, moving in and out of the ballroom as required, but without having to dance and act at one and the same time. Similarly, in Act II, the outdoor Japanese-lantern hung setting could be considered the picturesque retiring area from the indoor ballroom. More ambitious societies, on the other hand, might seek to emulate the original production and not only include the dances in the script, but also add country dances of their own, both before Acts and, possibly, at the end of the play. Pace and continuity should be considered essential ingredients for a successful production of this play, to which end it is recommended that the stage crew be dressed in costume similar to the servants and that the scene changes take place, wherever possible, around the actors and the action ensuring that it moves smoothly indoors and outdoors, from elegant drawing-room to formal park setting.

The play-scenes which are performed by the residents and guests at Mansfield Park in the second half of Act I are taken from August von Kotzebue's *Lovers' Vows*, translated from the German by Elizabeth Inchbald in 1798; the play referred to in Jane Austen's novel and which was a popular piece in England in the early part of the nineteenth century. It should be remembered that amateur theatricals were as popular then as they are today, and the actors who perform in Mr Yates's company should approach their parts as competent performers and not attempt to ham-up the play-within-the-play except, of course, as specified in the script.

Tom Bertram's drinking problems, leading to his eventual illness, while barely referred to in the dialogue, might be hinted at, particularly in Act II, by his occasional sly recourse to the contents of a hip-flask.

Despite some research, the rules governing Speculation, the card game referred to in Miss Austen's novel and which is played on stage in Act II, would seem to have been lost in the mists of time. Societies are therefore invited to invent their own simple rules involving the making and taking of tricks — which need be no more complicated than Snap.

Again, in the original production, an imitation dog was used for Pug, Lady Bertram's lap-dog — a device which is wholeheartedly recommended for all intended productions!

Willis Hall

Other plays by Willis Hall
published by Samuel French Ltd

Christmas Crackers
Jane Eyre (adapted from Charlotte Brontë)
Kidnapped at Christmas
The Long and the Short and the Tall
The Play of the Royal Astrologers
The Railwayman's New Clothes
A Right Christmas Caper
Treasure Island (musical adaptation from R. L. Stevenson)
Walk On, Walk On
The Water Babies (musical adaptation from Charles Kingsley)

Plays by Keith Waterhouse and Willis Hall
published by Samuel French Ltd

All Things Bright and Beautiful
Billy Liar
Celebration
Children's Day
Say Who You Are
Sponge Room *and* Squat Betty
Whoops-a-Daisy
Who's Who
Worzel Gummidge

ACT I

The Drawing-Room, Mansfield Park

Where Lady Bertram is discovered taking her ease on a chaise-longue, *cradling a pug dog in her lap, as Gipton, a housemaid, addresses the audience*

Gipton As somebody much cleverer than me once had the common-sense to mention: There's not so many men of large fortune in this world, as there are pretty women to deserve them — and certainly not in Northampton-shire ——

Lady Bertram tinkles a handbell

Yes, milady?
Lady Bertram Summon me a servant, Gipton.

During the following, Harkness, a butler, enters

Gipton Yes, milady. (*Back to the audience*) Well, why not? Why should her ladyship stir her sticks to cross a room and summon a servant when she can summon a servant to summon a servant at her behest?

During the following, Sir Thomas Bertram enters, kisses his wife and takes a seat

Harkness The comforts and consequences of living in a handsome house and with a very rich baronet for a husband. You rang, your ladyship?
Lady Bertram Pug needs his exercise.

During the following, Braithwaite, a second housemaid, enters

Harkness Yes, your ladyship. (*He takes the pug and moves out of Lady Bertram's earshot*) Pug is not alone in that particular. Lady Bertram has two sisters, both of whom aspired to marrying with similar advantage.

During the following, Mrs Norris and the Reverend Norris enter, nod at Sir Thomas and Lady Bertram and also seat themselves

Braithwaite (*taking up the narration*) No such good fortune. Miss Ward, the eldest sister, was obliged to be attached to the Reverend Mr Norris, a friend of her brother-in-law, with scarcely any private fortune.

Gipton and Braithwaite exit

Harkness The youngest sister, Frances Ward, fared worse, alas. She married, in the common phrase, to disoblige her family, by fixing on a Lieutenant of Marines, shorebound in Portsmouth — a man incapable of providing his wife with anything — apart from another mouth to feed each year ——

Harkness exits, shaking his head in disapproval

Mrs Norris — A husband unfit for active service, but not short on energy, it would appear, in the pursuit of weak company and strong drink. And our poor sister has allowed the brute to get her with child *again*?
Lady Bertram So she informs us.
Rev Norris Again!
Mrs Norris Her ninth lying-in.
Rev Norris Such a superfluity of children.
Sir Thomas Such a want, it seems, of almost everything else.
Lady Bertram She craves for our assistance. I shall arrange to have some money sent and some baby-linen.
Sir Thomas I shall despatch my most sincere regards — coupled with some timely advice for the husband.
Mr Norris I shall write a letter too, pointing out the folly of her conduct.
Lady Bertram She is our only sister — should we not do more?
Mrs Norris Supposing we were to undertake, between us, the upbringing of her eldest daughter, Fanny?
Lady Bertram An excellent suggestion! Send for the child immediately.
Sir Thomas Is that a good idea? There is our own brood to consider.

At which point, the four Bertram children: Tom, Edmund, Julia and Maria, hurtle through the room, shrieking and shouting. None of the present occupants appears to notice the children

Lady Bertram What have the children to do with the matter?
Sir Thomas Nought whatsoever — so far as Julia and Maria are concerned — I was thinking of Tom and Edmund. Supposing one of them should take a fancy to her?

Mrs Norris Do not let us be frightened from a good deed by a trifle, Sir Thomas.

Lady Bertram She is quite right. We should do everything we can.

Mrs Norris She is barely ten years old. Of all things upon earth, that is the least likely thing to happen. It is morally impossible. She will never be more to either than a sister.

Tom, Edmund, Julia and Maria hurtle through the room again, retracing their steps, shrieking and shouting

Again, they are totally ignored by the occupants

Lady Bertram I think we cannot do better.

Reverend Norris My dear, I think you are to be commended not only for your foresight but also for your compassion.

Mrs Norris Whatever I am able to do, I am always ready to do on behalf of those I love. I could not bear to see the poor child want, so long as I had a bit of bread to give her.

Lady Bertram And to which of us shall she come first? To you or us?

Mrs Norris Oh, but she could not come to us, sister. Not under any circumstances.

Sir Thomas Not come to you? Without children of your own, I had thought the girl would prove a welcome addition at the parsonage.

Mrs Norris And so she would — had it not been for Mr Norris's poor state of health. As it is, he could no more bear the noise of a child about the house than he could fly. Is it not so, my dear?

The Reverend Norris obliges with a small cough

Besides, you have the little white attic to keep her in. Much the best place for her. Not too far from your own girls and yet close enough to the servants' quarters to remind her of her station.

Lady Bertram It is settled then. For the time being, Fanny Price shall come to us.

Sir Thomas And let this be her home. God willing, we shall endeavour to do our duty by her.

Mrs Norris I shall write to our poor sister tomorrow.

The Lights dim on the drawing-room

The Reverend Norris and Mrs Norris move off in one direction, Harkness enters from another in a spot

Harkness Mrs Norris did not set pen to paper in vain. Mrs Price accepted
the offer gratefully — assuring her sisters that her daughter was a well-
disposed good-humoured girl, though somewhat delicate and puny. Fanny
Price endured the long journey safely — and was met at Northampton by
Mrs Norris who rejoiced in the credit of being first to welcome her.

The Lights come up on another area

*Mrs Norris enters, ushering in the ten-year-old Fanny Price. Fanny is
poorly dressed. She scarce dares raise her eyes to take in the splendour of
her surroundings. They are followed in by Gipton who is carrying a small
trunk*

Gipton I'd never set eyes before on anything so shy and timid. Such a pale,
drawn little creature with barely anything to call her own, poor lass. (*To
Fanny*) Is this all you've fetched with you?
Mrs Norris Go away, girl!

Gipton sets down the trunk and exits

*Mrs Norris helps Fanny take off her coat and bonnet. Fanny stands quite still,
frozen with fear*

Now, Fanny, remember everything that I have told you. A great deal will
depend upon your acquitting yourself well in the beginning. First impres-
sions are so important. So is carriage. Head up, stand straight and do hold
back those shoulders. This way.

Mrs Norris leads Fanny off as Braithwaite enters with a cake-stand

The Lights come up on the drawing-room area

Braithwaite With which, with Fanny's eyes still fixed on the floor and with
her shoulders drooping, Mrs Norris led her into the drawing-room, where
Sir Thomas, Lady Bertram and their children waited to meet her.

*The Bertrams assemble in the room as Braithwaite exits, then Mrs Norris
returns, leading in Fanny who is totally overawed*

Mrs Norris This is Fanny Price.
Sir Thomas Welcome to Mansfield Park. I am your uncle, Sir Thomas. This
is your aunt, the Lady Bertram. These are your cousins: Tom, Edmund,
Julia and Maria.

*The Bertram children study Fanny who has sat down, suddenly, on her own
trunk. She does not dare to raise her face and return their stares*

Maria Did you know, Mamma, that she has only two sashes in her entire wardrobe?

Julia She has been sent to us without a single plaything. We must search the nursery and find some old toys for her that we are done with.

Tom Were you aware, Papa, that she does not possess so much as a single word of French?

Mrs Norris I have spent the entire time since I collected her in trying to impress the girl of her good fortune. I have done my best to explain to her how she must prove her gratitude by good behaviour — and all she can do is snivel and hang her head.

Sir Thomas Has the girl been fed and watered since she departed Portsmouth? Provide her with a pastry, Edmund.

Edmund selects a small tart from the cake-stand and proffers it to Fanny

Fanny (*in a small voice*) No, thank you.

Maria Take it, cousin.

Tom Eat it, cousin.

Julia Do taste it.

Maria It's a gooseberry tart.

Julia It's very good.

Braithwaite Fanny took the plate and, with her relatives watching, managed no more than two small bites before dissolving into the tears which had never been far from her eyes.

Maria Isn't she odd?

Sir Thomas This is not at all a robust child. The travelling has probably been too much for her. I think that she would be well advised to go straight to bed.

Tom (*losing interest in his cousin*) Edmund, will you allow me to beat you handsomely again at bagatelle?

Edmund Only if I'm allowed to play without benefit of your continual and constant cheating when you add up the scores.

Tom and Edmund go off in one direction and Maria and Julia in another as Harkness enters

Sir Thomas Show Miss Price up to the white attic, Harkness. She is more than ready for her bed.

Harkness picks up Fanny's trunk and escorts her, as she continues to weep, out of the drawing-room

Mrs Norris This is not at all a promising beginning. I do hope that she is not a sulky child — if she is, she will have got it from her mother.

Lady Bertram We should make allowance for the fact that she has only just this morning been uprooted from her family — with all its faults, it was her home.

Sir Thomas Exactly so — and she has not had time, as yet, to realize how much better off she is than she was before.

Braithwaite enters

Mrs Norris Then we can only pray that it is not too long before that fact becomes apparent to her, Sir Thomas. Moderation in all things.

Braithwaite It would take time, however, for Fanny Price to become reconciled to leaving behind her home and family. For the moment, she was overwhelmed by Lady Bertram's silence, overawed by Sir Thomas's stern demeanour, and overcome by Mrs Norris's admonitions.

Braithwaite exits as Maria and Julia hasten on and approach Lady Bertram

Julia Mamma, did you know that our cousin cannot put the map of Europe together!

Maria Only think, Mamma, she does not know the principal rivers in Russia!

Julia She has never heard of Asia Minor!

Maria She does not know the difference between watercolours and crayons!

Julia Did you ever hear of anything so stupid?

Mrs Norris It is very bad, but you must not expect everybody to be as quick at learning or as clever as yourselves.

Maria But Aunt, she really is so very ignorant! It's years and years since Julia and I first learned to repeat the chronological order of the kings and queens of England.

Julia Fanny cannot recite a single one!

Mrs Norris My dears, it is not at all necessary that she should be as accomplished as yourselves. *Au contraire!* It is far more desirable that there should be a difference. Now, as you have both worked so very hard this morning, why don't you take yourselves out into the sun for a little while?

During the following, Gipton enters, followed by Braithwaite

Lady Bertram Well spoken, sister! I will be well satisfied with Fanny so long as she does not take to teasing poor Pug. I have only just got Julia to leave well alone. Have I not, my poor lambkin?

Gipton It wasn't only her aunts and uncles that were the cause of Fanny's sadness — Mansfield Park was much too grand a place for such a scrap of a girl ——

The Lights begin to cross-fade to Scene 2

Braithwaite — And though she did her best to go through one day after another and not appear ungrateful of all that was being done for her, she sobbed herself to sleep night after night.

Everyone exits

SCENE 2

The Schoolroom, Mansfield Park

Which will consist of no more than a blackboard and a small school chair which Fanny is sitting on, weeping copiously

Edmund enters, quietly, carrying a writing-box

Edmund Fanny, dear little cousin, what's brought this on? Are you ill? Has something — someone — angered you? Have you quarrelled with Maria and Julia?
Fanny No, no — not at all.

During the following, Gipton enters

Edmund Is it to do with anyone here at Mansfield Park? Or are you wishing you were back among your family and friends in Portsmouth?
Gipton Her sobs increased, informing him that he had touched upon the truth.
Edmund Poor Fanny. You are missing your mother. You will for a time. But you must try and take comfort in the knowledge that you are among friends and family here — who all love you and want to see you happy. Would it help to talk about home? About Portsmouth? Apart from your parents, Fanny, whom do you miss the most?
Fanny Mamma the most, and next to missing Mamma, I do miss William.
Edmund William? Which one is he?
Fanny My eldest brother. He is two years older than I am. He is my dearest, favourite brother and he is my very best friend.
Edmund And you are wondering if William is missing you as much as you are missing him?
Fanny Worse than that. I have been wondering if I will ever set eyes on him again?
Edmund You shall, you shall! But of course you shall! I am sure that he will write to you.

Fanny I am sure he will. But he said that first I was to write to him.

Edmund Well then! And when shall you do it?

Fanny I don't know. (*Again bursting into tears*) I haven't any paper.

Edmund (*opening his writing-box*) If that is your only problem, you shall have some instantly: pens, ink, everything that you require. Would it make you happy to write to William?

Fanny Yes, very.

Edmund Then you shall do it now. And I shall sit beside you, little cousin, and sharpen your pen for you whenever it is blunt. How's this? I shall send my cousin, William, a whole half guinea which we shall hide, for safe-keeping, underneath the sealing-wax — and you shall explain this to him in the letter. Would that please him, do you think? And, more important, would it please you to do so?

Fanny Both! Oh, Edmund, thank you, thank you! I cannot begin to know how to thank you.

Edmund By writing your letter to your brother, Fanny dear. How else?

Fanny applies herself to the task, casting occasional glances up into Edmund's face

Gipton enters, followed by Braithwaite

Gipton She felt that she had found herself a friend — and, from that day forward, Fanny grew more comfortable. The kindness of her cousin, Edmund, gave her better spirits with everyone else. Mansfield Park became less strange to her, and its occupants less formidable ——

Braithwaite — And if Fanny still remained a little frightened by Mrs Norris's pursed lips and strict attentions, at least she managed not to show that fear whenever her aunt walked into the room.

The Lights fade on the schoolroom

Everyone exits

As the stage clears, Harkness enters from one direction and Mrs Norris, wearing deepest mourning, enters from the opposite side

Harkness The first event of any importance in the family, which happened when Fanny was just sixteen, was the death of the Reverend Mr Norris.

Harkness exits

SCENE 3

The Grounds, Mansfield Park

*The Lights come up on an area of consecrated ground, represented by the
empty stage, on a dull and drizzly afternoon, where a group of black-garbed
Mourners are gathered under black umbrellas: Fanny, Edmund, Julia,
Maria, Tom, Sir Thomas, Lady Bertram and Mrs Grant. The burial service
is conducted by Dr Grant, a "short-necked apoplectic sort of fellow", in his
mid-forties — Mrs Grant is some years younger than her husband. During
the following, Mrs Norris crosses to join the Mourners*

Dr Grant ... Man that is born of woman hath but a short time to live and is
full of misery. He cometh up, and is cut down like a flower. He fleeth as
it were a shadow, and never continueth in one stay ... Earth to earth, ashes
to ashes, dust to dust, in sure and certain hope of the Resurrection to eternal
life. The grace of our Lord Jesus Christ, and the love of God and the
fellowship of the Holy Ghost be with us all evermore.
Mourners Amen.

*The funeral party breaks up and the Mourners take their leave of Dr Grant,
before embracing Mrs Norris, offering their condolences. Simultaneously,
the sun comes out as Gipton enters, carrying a straw hat and a small,
portable medicine chest. During the following, Harkness enters and Dr
Grant, Mrs Grant and Mrs Norris exit*

Gipton There were other departures too that year — though neither of them
had the awful finality of the Reverend Norris's leave-taking.
Harkness His Lordship deemed it expedient to go off to Antigua.

*The umbrellas have been taken down and the mourning discarded — except
by Mrs Norris*

Gipton Your medicine-box, your lordship.
Lady Bertram You will try not to contract any diseases too unpleasant in
the Indies, won't you, Sir Thomas?
Sir Thomas You may be sure that I shall not go out of my way to contract
anything, my dear — apart from a new estate manager — the current holder
of that office presenting me with more concern than he provides me with
profits.
Lady Bertram The very thought of your absence for an entire twelve-month
is too exhausting to be contemplated.
Sir Thomas Maria! Julia!

Maria and Julia approach their father

Maria Shall you be gone for a whole year, Papa?

Julia How shall we contrive to speed the time, sir, until your return?

Sir Thomas I do not doubt that, by combining your ingenuities, you will concoct some ideas on how to pass the weeks and months. (*Turning to Lady Bertram*) As soon as your sister is over her bereavement, Maria, you might have her turn her thoughts to finding suitable husbands for the pair of them. Thomas! Edmund!

His sons step forward

I shall trust to the both of you, and both of your judgements, to allow me to make my journey without fears for either of your sisters' conducts.

Tom I hope all goes well, sir, in Antigua.

Edmund God speed your safe return.

Sir Thomas Fanny!

Fanny approaches, shyly

How is Wilberforce?

Fanny Sir?

Sir Thomas Wilberforce — your favourite brother.

Fanny William, sir. He is well, sir. He is midshipman now, sir, in His Majesty's navy.

Sir Thomas Is he! Is he, by George! Then you must write him and tell him, from me, that he must come and visit you when he is granted shore leave.

Fanny (*a little over-excited at the prospect*) May I, Uncle? Oh, may I? I would like that! He would like that.

During the following, Harkness enters carrying a small sea-going trunk

Sir Thomas He may be surprised at the change he sees in you. On the other hand — the surprise may come in the discovery that his sister, although she is sixteen, is not much improved on the one he bade his goodbyes to when she was ten.

Harkness Then Sir Thomas turned his back on Fanny, leaving her close to tears again at his unexpected sudden rebuke.

Sir Thomas (*taking the hat and medicine-box*) Thank you, Gipton.

Sir Thomas exits, followed by Harkness, as Mrs Norris returns, having discarded her black veil and shawl but still wearing the black mourning dress

Gipton Mrs Norris was another on the move — out of the parsonage and into a small house close by Mansfield Park, where she consoled herself for the loss of her husband by considering that she could do very well without him.

What was a funeral is now become a garden-party

Mrs Norris Don't snivel, Fanny!

Dr Grant, having taken off his vestments, enters with Mrs Grant as Harkness returns. During the following, Mr Rushworth enters

Harkness And as Mrs Norris moved out of the parsonage, the Reverend Doctor Grant moved in — with his wife who was about fifteen years his junior. And there was another newcomer to the county ...

Mr Rushworth, a heavily-built young man, pleasant enough but not over-burdened with intelligence, is standing in the centre of a semi-circle of Bertrams and their guests. All eye him keenly

Lady Bertram What is that young man's name?
Fanny Why, he is Mr Rushworth, Aunt Bertram.
Lady Bertram Is he a well set-up young man?
Fanny Exceedingly so. He has recently inherited Sotherton Court.
Lady Bertram Has he indeed! I have never been blessed with both the energy and the inclination to visit Sotherton — but I believe it is considered one of the finest estates in the county?
Fanny I understand that too, Aunt Bertram.
Mrs Norris As far as I can decide, sister, on a very short acquaintance, Mr Rushworth would appear to be precisely the young man to deserve Maria — while Maria, as you and I are both aware, has all of those qualities and accomplishments best suited to make any young man of substance happy.

Maria, who is of a similar mind, is displaying her charms to Mr Rushworth at a distance, flirting with him outrageously

Lady Bertram One can only beg leave to wonder, sister, why they have not as yet been introduced?
Dr Grant How old is the elder of the Bertram girls?
Mrs Grant Maria will be twenty-one this year.
Dr Grant She has reached an age then when she should be beginning to think of marriage as a duty.
Mrs Grant And Mr Rushworth, I understand, is so taken with the idea of marriage that he cannot wait to fall in love.

Maria (*still gazing covetously at Mr Rushworth*) I can see nothing disagreeable in any way with Mr Rushworth, Julia.

Julia Marry him, Maria, and you'll not only become mistress of Sotherton Court and an enviable house in town — you'll also own cupboard after cupboard full of fashionable gowns in both of them!

Maria I can see nothing disagreeable in any way with Mr Rushworth — either in his person, his properties or his personal fortune.

Edmund The only thing he does seem short on is intelligence — if that man did not have twelve thousand a year, he would be a very stupid fellow.

Mrs Norris leads Maria up to Mr Rushworth

The others exit. During the following, Harkness enters

Mrs Norris Mr Rushworth, may I introduce my niece, Miss Bertram? Maria, this is Mr Rushworth.

Maria It's a pleasure to meet you, Mr Rushworth.

Mr Rushworth The pleasure, Miss Bertram, is entirely — quite utterly and delightfully — all mine.

Harkness Hooked, gaffed and safely landed.

Mrs Norris, Mr Rushworth and Maria exit

SCENE 4

The Ballroom, Mansfield Park

Which may be represented by a chandelier, with several chairs on the periphery of the dance floor. A moonlit terrace may be visible to the rear

Lady Bertram sits at the side of the dance floor, with Fanny in attendance at her side

The music of a country dance strikes up during the following and couples enter, dancing: Mr Rushworth and Maria; Edmund and Julia; Dr Grant and Mrs Grant; Mrs Norris and Tom. Two newcomers also grace the scene and are the centre of attention — they are Mrs Grant's brother and sister, Henry and Mary Crawford. (See the Production Note on page vi)

Harkness The long-awaited summer ball which was held to celebrate the engagement of Miss Bertram and Mr Rushworth, was considered, by all of those invited to attend, to be the outstanding event of the season ——

Gipton While those that didn't get invited were hardly reckoned worthy of opinions.

Conversation takes place as the dance continues. As is customary in country dancing, the couples may change partners. Sometimes, it may be considered appropriate to freeze the action while words are spoken to emphasize a point

Julia Who is that devastatingly desirable man?

Edmund And who is the delightful young woman at his side?

Mrs Norris Mr Henry Crawford and Miss Mary Crawford — Mrs Grant's brother and sister.

Lady Bertram Are they well set-up?

Julia He has a good estate in Norfolk.

Edmund She has twenty thousand pounds — or thereabouts.

Lady Bertram While I am in possession of a daughter sorely in need of a husband and two sons sadly lacking wives.

Henry (*to Mrs Grant*) I do find the Miss Bertrams exceedingly desirable, sister.

Mrs Grant I hope for both their sakes, and yours, brother, that you have a preference for Julia.

Henry Which one is Maria?

Mr Rushworth I am entirely in a quandary, my dearest one, with regard to Sotherton Court. Immediately after we are married, you must seek out some person who might landscape me properly. I have some seven hundred acres that cry out for attention.

Maria The moment we are married, my love, and I hold the domestic purse-strings, I shall endeavour to seek out the most expensive landscaper in the land.

Mrs Grant (*to Henry*) Julia is the one that is entirely available.

Dr Grant A nice, good-natured and accomplished girl.

Mrs Grant Henry, you shall marry Julia — she will make you very happy.

Henry Thank you for the thought.

Mary My dear sister, if you can persuade Henry to marry, you must have the address of a Frenchwoman — all that England has to offer has been tried already. Our brother is the most horrible flirt.

Mrs Grant I hope that you will remember, Henry, that Maria Bertram is engaged. Her choice is made.

Henry Yes, and alas I fear that I desire her the more because of it. An engaged woman is always more agreeable than one that is unattached. All is safe with a lady engaged — no harm can be done.

Mrs Grant Mary, what are we to do with him?

Mary We must leave him to look after his own affairs.

Henry And you may have my solemn assurance, sisters, that I shall do my
very utmost to desire Julia the most — if only to make you happy.

*By which time, the dance has ended, though the music may continue in the
background*

During the following, Braithwaite enters with a tray of punch

Lady Bertram If I were you, Mr Rushworth, when you have laid hands upon
your landscape gardener, you will have him put in a shrubbery. One likes
to get out into a shrubbery in fine weather.
Mr Rushworth A shrubbery would seem an excellent suggestion, ma'am.
It would replace an entire avenue of birch trees I intend to have taken down.
It quite obscures the view from the terrace.
Maria How very clever, did you think of that yourself? Do you have other
thoughts?

*Mr Rushworth shrugs modestly in answer to the first question, but finds the
second question beyond him*

Fanny (*to Edmund*) Cut down an entire avenue? What a pity! Might not Mr
Rushworth be prevailed upon to give more thought to such a serious
decision?
Edmund If we are to depend upon Mr Rushworth's powers of thought,
Fanny — I fear the avenue stands poor chance, if any.
Henry (*to Mary*) Perhaps I shall do my level best to break both their hearts.
Why is it that I always want the most that which I cannot have?
Mary I would have said that you want every woman you set eyes upon.
Henry At least I am not afraid to admit it, sister. Shall you tell me now which
of the Bertram brothers you are scheming after?

*Mary looks across at where Tom and Edmund, having obtained drinks from
Braithwaite, are delivering them to, firstly, Mrs Norris and, secondly, Fanny*

Mary They are both of them fine young men — and both of them seem well-
mannered. The elder one, I understand, has spent much time in London
and seems to be a livelier and more gallant person. I had felt an early
presentiment that I should like the eldest best.
Henry And the fact that he will come into a baronetcy, to say nothing of
inheriting Mansfield Park, did not serve to influence your decision?
Mary Not at all.
Henry While the knowledge that the younger brother is destined for a parish
priesthood does not detract in any way from his desirability?

Mary I did not know that he was.

Henry So I understand.

Mary Poor man! Perhaps I shall take a leaf from your book, brother, and break two hearts rather than the one.

Henry (*who has been looking across at Fanny*) Not every woman I set eyes upon — who is the sad-eyed, whey-faced creature cowering in the corner?

Mary That will be Fanny Price — the Bertrams' poor relation.

Henry Thank heavens for that!

Mary That she is without a fortune?

Henry That I feel no attraction in that direction whatsoever.

Braithwaite At this point, Henry Crawford invites Maria Bertram on to the quiet seclusion of the moonlit terrace to teach her to waltz — a brave new dance arrived from Vienna.

Henry has done just that and will either take Maria out on to the terrace, or off stage

Edmund Fanny, my dear?

Fanny (*hopefully*) Yes, Edmund?

Edmund Would you excuse me while I ask Miss Crawford if she might care to dance?

Fanny (*crestfallen, having expected that same invitation herself*) Of course.

Mr Rushworth, arriving back from the drinks tray with two glasses of punch, is surprised at finding Maria gone. He approaches Fanny

Mr Rushworth Miss Price, do you think that you might care to ...

Fanny (*rising, expecting another invitation to dance*) Thank you, Mr Rushworth.

But Mr Rushworth is also offering her a glass of punch and Fanny finds herself juggling a glass in either hand

Mr Rushworth My pleasure entirely.

Fanny I have just been remarking to my cousin, Mr Rushworth, that I would very much like to see Sotherton Court before the avenue of birch trees is cut down.

Mr Rushworth, who has been jealously watching Maria and Henry on the terrace, does not appear to have heard

Mr Rushworth Tell me, Miss Price, are you an admirer of this Mr Crawford?

Fanny I do not find him handsome, Mr Rushworth.

Mr Rushworth Handsome! Nobody could think such an undersized fellow handsome. He is not five foot nine. I should not wonder if he was not more than five foot eight.

Fanny If you say so, Mr Rushworth.

Mr Rushworth You were saying, a moment ago, that you might care to see Sotherton Court at some time in the near future?

Fanny I should certainly like to.

Mr Rushworth Your cousins have expressed a similar desire. I don't doubt that a carriage to accommodate everyone could be arranged for tomorrow.

Fanny That would be delightful, Mr Rushworth. I have heard so much said about Sotherton Court.

Mrs Norris (*who has been eavesdropping*) I have been told that Sotherton is the noblest old place in the entire world. I should dearly love to see it too.

Mr Rushworth It wants improvement, ma'am, beyond anything. I have seven hundred acres and each one cries out for improvement.

Mrs Norris And Lady Bertram also, I feel sure, would welcome an opportunity of looking over her future son-in-law's estate.

Lady Bertram What is that that I would be pleased to do, sister?

Mrs Norris Mr Rushworth is arranging to take a party of us to see Sotherton Court.

Lady Bertram I am indebted for the invitation, Mr Rushworth. Alas though, in my own case it is quite out of the question.

Mrs Norris Her ladyship suffers most dreadfully from fatigue, Mr Rushworth.

Lady Bertram I am a martyr to fatigue, Mr Rushworth. It was as much as I could bear this afternoon to sit out in the garden.

Mrs Norris It is the heat that is to blame for it.

Lady Bertram Sitting and calling out to Pug, in an attempt to keep him from the flowerbeds, was almost too much for me.

Mr Rushworth Perhaps we should postpone your own visit to Sotherton, Lady Bertram, until the autumn when the days are cooler?

Lady Bertram Summer to winter — travel is a pleasure I am forced to deny myself.

Mrs Norris Your presence will be sadly missed, sister — and such a pity, Fanny, that you shall also be required to remain behind at Mansfield Park.

Mr Rushworth Oh, but Miss Price has been invited.

Edmund (*having overheard some of the above*) There can be no doubt of there being room for Fanny?

Mrs Norris There can be no question of Fanny going. Your mother cannot manage without her.

Edmund You can have no reason, ma'am, for wishing Fanny not to be included in the party? If you could do without her, you would not wish to keep her at home?

Lady Bertram To be sure not, Edmund, but I must have her here to fetch and carry. I cannot do without her.

Edmund You can — if I stay home with you, as I intend to do.

Maria It will seem very odd, Edmund, that you shall be staying home instead of Fanny.

Edmund It is decided.

Julia I'm sure she ought to be very much obliged to you.

Tom Edmund — there's no need for you to stay at home, for I have to be at home tomorrow on my own account. I am expecting the arrival of a friend. I shall attend to all your needs, ma'am.

Lady Bertram Provided there is someone to provide for me. I should not care to be marooned with nobody to call upon for assistance, excepting servants.

Mrs Norris (*glancing balefully at Fanny, believing her to somehow be responsible for these alterations*) Very well, very well! Just as you choose. Settle it your own way. I am sure I do not care about it.

Fanny Thank you, Tom. And thank you, Edmund, for the kindness of the offer.

Edmund I knew how much you wanted to see Sotherton — and I have already seen it.

Mr Rushworth It is agreed then, is it, who is to come and who to remain behind? I must confess that I have not yet fully comprehended whom I shall be welcoming.

Gipton At which point, the music begins again, and the dancers return to the floor with different partners. Fanny, to her ultimate delight, finds herself dancing with Edmund.

With the exception of Mrs Norris and Lady Bertram, the dancers form themselves into a circle and perform a more energetic version of the country dance, at the end of which they exit

Mrs Norris I think, ma'am, that we shall see some happy faces now. It is quite delightful, is it not, to see young people so properly happy, well suited and so much the thing!

Lady Bertram I cannot but contemplate Sir Thomas's delight when he comes back from Antigua and is able to bless the match in person.

Mrs Norris Mr Rushworth and Maria have set a good example. Such things are catching.

Lady Bertram Mr Crawford and Julia ... ?

Mrs Norris Do you see symptoms there?

Lady Bertram They would make a pretty match. What is Mr Crawford's property?

Mrs Norris A good estate in Norfolk and four thousand a year.

Lady Bertram Those who have not more must be satisfied with what they have.

Lady Bertram and Mrs Norris exit as Gipton enters followed by Braithwaite

Gipton The next day, after breakfast, Edmund, Mary Crawford, Maria, Mrs Norris and Fanny were inside the barouche with Henry Crawford on the driving seat and Julia sitting happily in pride of place beside him.

The Lights fade

Braithwaite The trip to Sotherton was on!

Everyone exits

SCENE 5

The Drive, Mansfield Park

Which may be represented by an empty stage, as Harkness enters, followed by Tom and Lady Bertram

Harkness Lady Bertram, her presence adding to the importance of the occasion, had walked down the drive to see them off.

Tom Mamma, I am totally at your service.

Lady Bertram How nice. Allow me to lean upon you, Tom — bidding one's goodbyes is so strenuous.

They turn to move indoors

A young man, Mr Yates, enters, followed by Harkness, carrying a large trunk

Mr Yates Mr Bertram!

Tom Mr Yates! Mamma, this is Mr Yates.

Lady Bertram I am in no condition to arouse enthusiasm at the entrance of a total stranger. Tom, I'm so tired I shall meet Mr Yates later.

Lady Bertram exits

Tom and Mr Yates embrace, enthusiastically

Mr Yates Mr Bertram!

Tom Mr Yates! I had not expected you so soon.

Mr Yates You have had my letter?

Tom That you were leaving Lord Ravenshaw's estate at Ecclesford earlier than was expected, yes — but even so I had still not expected your arrival here before this afternoon.

Mr Yates Alas, I travelled quickly — borne upon the wings of disappointment.

Tom The entertainment was cut short, you said, by a sudden bereavement?

Mr Yates Bereavement, yes — but upon my word, it was no ordinary entertainment that was thus ended. We were within two days of opening, Tom, when Lord Ravenshaw's first cousin, the Right Honourable, keeled over during the lobster, clawed at the tablecloth, slipped beneath the table — and instantly expired. It was extremely inconsiderate of him. We were forced to cancel our performance. Can you comprehend our disappointment. Upon my word, Tom — we were within two days!

Tom Of opening?

Mr Yates *Lovers' Vows.*

Tom *Lovers' Vows?*

Mr Yates August von Kotzebue's *Lovers' Vows*. Imagine the bustle! The excitement! I was to have given my Count Cassel. A trifling part, I must admit, and such a one as I would not take on again, should opportunity arise — but, upon my word, Tom, if you could only have seen me in that costume, on that stage!

Tom (*finally comprehending*) You were appearing in a play.

Mr Yates Isn't everyone this year? "You cannot find better work or better taste!" That's Count Cassel. Don't tell me you have never held a theatrical party at Mansfield Park?

Tom Never.

Mr Yates My dear, good friend — believe me, there is nothing so exciting or so pleasurable upon this earth.

Tom Even if we so desired, I am sure that my father would not approve the venture ... On the other hand, Lord Bertram is abroad.

Mr Yates Upon my word! You cannot find better work ——

Tom puts his arm through Mr Yates's

Tom ⎱
Mr Yates ⎰ (*together*) — or better taste!

They exit

Harkness They linked arms, conspiratorially, and went indoors — followed
by small butler carrying large trunk.

Harkness exits

The Lights fade

Braithwaite enters in a spot

Braithwaite Meanwhile, at Sotherton Court, Edmund, Mary and Fanny had
landed in the wilderness, a planted wood of about two acres, chiefly of larch
and laurel and beech cut down — and though laid out with too much
regularity, was all darkness and shade which they could only walk and
admire ...

The Lights come up on the next scene

Scene 6

The Wilderness, Sotherton Court

*Which consists of an open space on the perimeter of a wood and overlooking
the formal park which is bordered, at the rear, by a decorative iron fence.
There is a gate in the fence. There are a couple of garden benches*

Edmund and Mary enter, followed by Fanny

Braithwaite At length, Miss Crawford broke the silence.
Mary So you are to be a clergyman, Mr Bertram? You surprise me.
Edmund Why? I must take up some profession — my brother will inherit
Mansfield Park — and surely you cannot see me as a lawyer or a soldier
or a sailor?
Mary (*choosing to ignore the question*) How cool it is here in the shade —
and so delightfully tranquil too. I do hope that this is not a part of Sotherton
that Mr Rushworth has his heart set on improving.
Fanny Speaking of Mr Rushworth, Miss Crawford, we seem to have left him
and the others far behind. Shall we stay here a while and wait for them?
Mary I am sure that they would soon catch up with us, Miss Price, if such
was their desire. Perhaps they may have other matters on their minds?
Edmund It is not because you are tired, is it, Fanny, that you suggest that we
bide our time?

Fanny I wonder that I should be tired with only walking in this sweet wood
— but, if it is not disagreeable to you, I should soon like to rest for a little
while.

Edmund My dear Fanny, how thoughtless of me! (*He draws her arm inside
his own*) And perhaps my other companion may also do me the honour of
taking an arm?

Mary Thank you, but I am not at all tired. (*Nevertheless, she takes his arm*)
I cannot imagine why I am not so — for we must have walked at least a mile,
would you not say?

Edmund No more than half that distance, Miss Crawford, at the very most.

Mary But we have walked all through Mr Rushworth's "wilderness", as he
refers to it, along a path which has taken all kinds of twists and turns. I am
sure, Mr Bertram, that we have walked all of a mile and more.

*They pause in their stroll and Edmund looses his arm from Fanny's and
consults his watch. Fanny crosses and sits*

Edmund Then allow me to see. We have been in the wood for fifteen
minutes exactly. You would not suggest that we are walking four miles to
the hour?

Mary (*taking her arm from his*) Pray do not attack me with your watch. A
watch is always too fast or too slow. I will not be dictated to, Mr Bertram,
by a watch.

Edmund You are tired, Fanny — and I hold myself entirely to blame. I have
made you walk too far too fast.

Fanny No, Edmund.

Edmund And I say, yes, Fanny. All exercise fatigues her.

Mary If the poor girl is entirely exhausted, it would not surprise me in the
least. There is nothing in the world so tiring as the manner in which we have
spent this morning — being escorted around a sprawling house — having
to murmur one's approval at items to which one would not normally give
a second glace.

Fanny I shall be rested soon. I find nothing more refreshing than to sit in the
shade on a sunny afternoon and look out across a park.

Mary I find quite the opposite. Resting tires me completely — (*looking back
the way they have come*) — and that fence, in my opinion, spoils the view.

Edmund If you will turn your gaze along the fence, Miss Crawford, you will
realize that you were wrong. You can see the house from here and see that
it is only half a mile away, if that.

Mary I will admit that I was mistaken in my first assessment, Mr Bertram
— it is not a mile away, it is a mile and more.

Edmund No, Miss Crawford, half a mile at the very most, I do assure you.
The eyes do not lie.

Mary Precisely — and mine tell me that it is an immense distance, Mr Bertram. They tell me that at a glance.

Edmund Then allow the fence-posts to prove it to you. The largest ones are set, you will agree with me, approximately twenty feet apart ——

Mary Mr Bertram, I implore you! First you set out to confuse me with your watch and now you seek to confound me with arithmetical argument.

Edmund Miss Crawford, we can settle it easily and without further discussion.

Mary Nothing would please me more, Mr Bertram.

Edmund I cannot quarrel with you on that count.

Mary Very well. We shall stroll back as far as the end of the fence and back again. If it takes us more than several minutes at the very most, I will allow that you are right and I am wrong.

Fanny (*rising*) I will come with you.

Edmund You will no nothing of the kind, Fanny.

Mary We could not contemplate allowing you to further tax yourself, Miss Price.

Fanny But I am rested now.

Edmund You must allow me, Fanny, to be the best judge of that. No, you shall stay here and rest a little while longer.

Fanny (*sitting down again*) Yes, Edmund.

Mary You will feel all the better for doing so, Miss Price.

Edmund (*to Mary*) Well?

Mary If I am allowed to hold the watch.

Edmund (*giving her his watch*) I was about to voice that very proposition.

Mary And not too fast, Mr Bertram. I must be allowed to set the pace.

Edmund As slowly as you like, Miss Crawford. Fanny, we will still be back before you realize we are gone.

Edmund and Mary exit

Fanny rises, watches them go and then sits down again, despondent

Harkness enters

Harkness She watched them till they had disappeared, and listened till all sound of them had ceased. Then, she was left to think with pleasure of her cousin's care, but with great regret that she was not stronger. A quarter of an hour — twenty minutes — passed away, and Fanny was still thinking of Edmund, Miss Crawford and herself, when she heard voices and feet approaching.

Harkness exits as Henry, Maria and Mr Rushworth enter

Henry Miss Price! Are you abandoned?

Mr Rushworth How comes this?

Maria Fanny, where are Edmund and Miss Crawford?

Fanny They have gone on a little way. I had been suffering some slight fatigue and so I stayed behind to rest.

Maria Then they did desert you?

Fanny Not at all. They are coming back directly.

Henry My poor Miss Price, you would have done better to have stayed with us.

Fanny We did not know where you were. We came into the wood believing that you were close behind us.

Mr Rushworth It was we, Miss Price, that could not conceive where you had gone. One moment we were all one group — a moment later we were not. The three of you had raced on ahead while the other Miss Bertram and Mrs Norris lagged behind. We three were in a muddle in the middle.

Maria Mr Crawford has been so kind, cousin, as to offer to give us his advice on such improvements as might be undertaken at Sotherton once Mr Rushworth and myself are one.

Mr Rushworth God speed that day, Miss Bertram!

Maria Meanwhile though, Mr Crawford, I am sure that we should be obliged to you for any suggestions you might have?

Mr Rushworth Obliged, indeed — oh, most obliged.

Henry Whatever I might manage on your behalf, Miss Bertram, you may be sure I shall be more than happy to perform.

Mr Rushworth I don't know whether you may have heard me mention it, Miss Price, but I have some seven hundred acres, not reckoning the water-meadows. So you will realize that there is much that needs to be done.

Maria So many untouched areas hungering for attention, Mr Crawford, that it would seem time wasted not to make an instant start. Would you not say so, Mr Rushworth?

Mr Rushworth Whatever would make you happy, Miss Bertram, would be my wish also.

Henry As far as landscaping goes, Mr Rushworth, there is a Mr Repton whom some people seem to hold in high regard.

Fanny I have heard of Mr Repton, Mr Crawford. Would you yourself recommend him?

Mr Rushworth I have heard of Mr Repton myself, often. It had occurred to me, only last week in fact, to invite him here to Sotherton.

Henry On the other hand though, there are many that consider Repton's handiwork dull.

Mr Rushworth Dull, dull — extremely dull. I have heard it said a score of times — which is why I dismissed the possibility the moment that it crossed my mind.

Maria Then if you were in Mr Rushworth's place, Mr Crawford, you would seek assistance somewhere else?

Henry Ah! Were I in Mr Rushworth's place, Miss Bertram, which unhappily I am not, I would first see how much I might achieve myself before I sought any outside help.

Maria Would you indeed? I'm sure your personal attentions would be very much appreciated. And where, exactly, do you think you might begin?

Henry I would first seek out a vantage point. (*He points out through the iron fence*) Possibly from atop that knoll over there. (*He tries the gate*) What a pity. It is locked.

Maria That will not present a problem, Mr Crawford. Mr Rushworth has the key.

Mr Rushworth Ah!

Maria You do have a key?

Mr Rushworth Ah! I do have a key indeed, my dear. In fact, I have two keys. Alas, I don't have either one of them on my person.

Maria You did not bring one with you?

Mr Rushworth Not on this particular occasion. I only wish I had. I had been very near thinking before we left the house that I should bring it with me. I gave it very serious consideration. And I can give you my very solemn assurance that I shall never think to come this way again without it.

Maria Which does not solve this present evil.

Mr Rushworth Not at all. You have your heart set upon passing through to the other side?

Maria If Mr Crawford is to be allowed to grant us the benefit of his opinion — which he has very kindly offered to do — I do think that we should help him to do so.

Henry It is not of any immediate importance. Some other time. Or, perhaps, we might approach the knoll from a different direction?

Maria Not without a great deal of inconvenience.

Mr Rushworth We need to return as far as we have walked already — and more — and then set off on another path.

Maria It would be easier, would it not, for one of us to go back to the house and collect the key while the rest of us wait here?

Mr Rushworth It would only be fair and right if that person were to be me?

Maria Fair and right.

Henry Quite so.

Mr Rushworth I was the person who left the key behind. I am the person who knows where the key is kept. You may be sure, in order not to inconvenience you further, I shall make all haste. Miss Price, if you will excuse me — Mr Crawford, Miss Bertram.

Maria We shall expect you shortly.

Henry You may be sure on it!

Mr Rushworth sets off, in haste, back the way they came

Embarrassed by their flirting, Fanny contrives to keep out of Maria's and Henry's eyelines as the scene continues

Henry It is the best thing that could be done — considering the circumstances.

Maria Yes, it is the only thing — considering the circumstances. Tell me, Mr Crawford, do you not think that Sotherton Court is almost beyond improvement? Truthfully, do you not find the place far worse than you expected?

Henry Truthfully, Miss Bertram, I do not think that I shall ever see Sotherton again with so much pleasure as I do at this particular moment.

Maria You are too much a man of the world, Mr Crawford, not to see with the eyes of the world. If other people think Sotherton improved, I have no doubt that you will.

Henry I am afraid that I am not quite so much the man of the world as might be good for me in some instances. My feelings are not quite so fickle as one finds with men of the world, Miss Bertram.

Maria You seemed to enjoy the drive very much this morning. You and Julia were laughing all the way.

Henry Were we? Yes, I believe we were. Your sister loves to laugh.

Maria You think her more light-hearted than I am?

Henry More easily amused, perhaps.

Maria I believe I am as lively as Julia, Mr Crawford. But I have more on my mind at present.

Henry Undoubtedly — and there are occasions when high spirits are entirely out of place. But your future promises fair, Miss Bertram, and you have a very smiling scene in front of you.

Maria Do you mean literally or figuratively, Mr Crawford? Literally I conclude. Yes, certainly, the sun is shining and the park looks cheerful. Except that that iron fence gives me a feeling of being shut in. "I cannot get out," as the starling said.

Henry Pity the poor starling.

Maria tries the gate's handle

Maria It is not locked, Mr Crawford.

Henry Is it not?

Maria No. It is open.

Henry (*trying the handle himself, several times*) I swear to you that it seemed so. I was mistaken. Look — sometimes the lock catches, sometimes it does not.

Maria I believe you, Mr Crawford. I doubt that Mr Rushworth will be amused.

Henry At least you are not caged in any longer. The starling, should it so desire, can seek its freedom. Unless, of course, you feel that you must wait upon the return of Mr Rushworth.

Maria No. He will quickly catch us up. He will be back before we are out of sight.

Henry Or else, Miss Price will be so good as to tell him where we are gone. He will find us near that knoll, Miss Price, inside the grove of oak trees on the top of it.

Fanny Do you not think it would be wise to wait for Mr Rushworth, Maria? He will not be pleased to find that you have gone on without him.

Maria He will not be cross, cousin, if you explain to him exactly what has happened.

Fanny Maria, I do not think that you should go through that gate.

Maria Too late, cousin. I am through it. Goodbye!

Maria moves off with Henry

Fanny hastens across to the gate which, curiously, is locked again. Henry had spoken the truth: the lock does catch on some occasions

Fanny Maria! *Maria!* (*She crosses to a bench and sits*)

After several moments, Julia enters, hot and flustered

Julia Hey-day — and a fine day this one seems to be turning into!

Fanny Maria said that somehow you had been left behind with Aunt Norris?

Julia Do not mention Maria to me, miss! Maria contrived to have me left behind with Aunt Norris — and with Mr Rushworth's mother! Where is Maria? Where is everyone?

Fanny Maria and Mr Crawford have walked on towards that wooded knoll. Edmund and Miss Crawford went back for a stroll in the wood and should have been back some time ago. Mr Rushworth has gone back to the house.

Julia I passed Mr Rushworth some minutes since, hastening towards the house as if his life depended upon it. He barely took time to pause and mutter something that concerned a key.

Fanny To open that gate. Mr Crawford and Maria were anxious to overlook the house and grounds from an advantageous position.

Julia Oh?

Fanny In order that Mr Crawford might advise Mr Rushworth with regard to improving the estate.

Julia (*trying the gate which opens at her touch*) But the gate is not locked?

Fanny It seemed to be locked. It seems it catches. Sometimes it seems as if it is locked; sometimes not.

Julia (*opening and closing the gate again*) There is nothing at all amiss with the lock.

Fanny I promise you, Julia, it was shut fast before.

Julia And they have gone on to the knoll, you say, having sent Mr Rushworth back to fetch a key to fit a lock that is not closed. A pretty trick upon my word! I cannot see them anywhere. How long have they been gone?

Fanny No more than a minute or two before you came.

Julia They cannot be very far off. I'll soon catch up with them. (*She tries the gate again*) It's locked!

Fanny That is exactly how it was before.

Julia It's locked!

Fanny Mr Rushworth will be back in a moment, cousin, with the key.

Julia I do not propose to wait for Mr Rushworth, Fanny. I have had my fill today of Rushworths. It is not long now since I escaped from Mr Rushworth's mother! Such a penance I have endured while you have sat here enjoying yourself! I was obliged to endure Mrs Rushworth's prattle, while Aunt Norris prattled with the housekeeper. But Mrs Rushworth's son I do intend to escape from ...

Julia has discovered a loose railing — or perhaps a missing railing that has been hidden by hanging lichen — providing her with room to squeeze through

Fanny You must not try to go through there, Julia! You will hurt yourself against those spikes; you will tear your gown; you had best not try!

But Julia succeeds and stands, flushed with success on the other side of the fence

Julia Thank you, dear Fanny, but I and my gown are alive and well. Goodbye!

Julia sets off in the direction taken by Henry and Maria

Fanny watches her go

Mr Rushworth enters, hot and flustered but brandishing the key to the gate

Mr Rushworth Where are they?

Fanny They have gone on to the wooded knoll.

Mr Rushworth Gone on to the wooded knoll?

Fanny They desired me to stay. My cousin Maria charged me to say that you would find them at the knoll or thereabouts.

Mr Rushworth But I have been back to the house to fetch this key.

Fanny Yes. The gate, which Mr Crawford deemed to be locked, proved to be not locked at all.

Mr Rushworth I have run, without pause, both there and back.

Fanny Your journey has not been altogether wasted. The gate has somehow locked itself again. My cousin Julia has just been forced to squeeze herself between the railings.

Mr Rushworth turns the handle and the gate swings open

Mr Rushworth She had no need to — the gate is open.

Fanny They cannot have gone far. You will quickly find them.

Mr Rushworth I do not think that I shall try.

Fanny I'm sorry. You have been most unlucky.

Mr Rushworth I do think that they might have waited for me.

Fanny It was Maria's wish that you should follow her.

Mr Rushworth I should not have had to follow her if she had waited for me. I cannot imagine why she allows herself to suffer that man's company. I was right — he is not much more than a fraction over five foot seven. If I had made any difficulty about going for the key, there might have been some excuse, but I set off the very moment that she said she wanted it.

Fanny No-one could have been more obliging, Mr Rushworth, I am sure.

Mr Rushworth In my opinion, Miss Price, these Crawfords are no addition to our circle. We managed very well before they came.

Fanny It is a pity, Mr Rushworth, that you should not join them. They were hoping to find a better view there of the park, and will be thinking how it may be improved. Nothing could be settled in that particular without your presence.

Mr Rushworth Well, if you really think that I ought to go ... And it would be foolish, after all my to-and-froing after the key, not to pursue the matter ...

Mr Rushworth goes through the gate and sets off in pursuit of the others

Fanny watches him go, then sits

Mrs Norris enters. She is carrying a basket of vegetables, two wrapped cheeses and a small basket of pheasant's eggs

Mrs Norris Taking your ease again then, Fanny? You have had a fine day today and no mistake — nothing but pleasure in it from beginning to end.

Fanny Yes, Aunt Norris.

Mrs Norris Mrs Whitaker is a treasure! I did no more than express my admiration for the kitchen garden — chancing to mention, in passing, how poorly my own small plot had fared this year — and the dear lady insisted on my having these. Will you take it, Fanny? (*She hands Fanny the basket* *of vegetables*) And this is a whole cream cheese — similar to the one, you may remember, that I was complimentary over during lunch. I also happened to observe to Mrs Whitaker that our local dairy's cheese of late has been singularly disappointing — and she was adamant on my having one from here. (*She gives the cheese to Fanny*) And these are pheasant's eggs that Mrs Whitaker emphatically forced upon me. Mansfield Park, as I explained to her in conversation, has been quite bereft of pheasant this year. I shall get the dairymaid to set them under her first spare hen. If they come good, I shall move them to my own house — if I can come across someone kind enough to loan me a coop. (*She gives the basket of eggs to Fanny*) Come, Fanny!

Mrs Norris and Fanny exit the way they came

The Lights fade

Harkness enters in a spot and begins the narration to cover the scene change. Gipton and Braithwaite enter, each in their own spot, to join in

During the following, Lady Bertram, Mrs Norris, Mary, Fanny, Edmund, Maria, Julia, Mr Rushworth, Henry, Tom and Mr Yates enter and assemble c

Harkness It was a beautiful evening, mild and still and moonlit. The day at Sotherton, with all its imperfections, afforded the Miss Bertrams much more agreeable feelings than they derived, over the coming months, from the letters from Sir Thomas in Antigua.

Gipton Maria was much more to be pitied than Julia, for her father's return would mean her union with the man that she had chosen for her husband. It was a gloomy prospect, and all that she could do was throw a mist over it, and hope that when the mist cleared away, she would see something else.

Braithwaite November was the black month fixed for Sir Thomas's return.

Gipton It would hardly be early in November though, there were generally delays, a bad passage or something.

Harkness It would probably be the middle of November at least.

Gipton The middle of November was three months off.

Braithwaite Three months comprised thirteen weeks.

Gipton A great deal might happen in thirteen weeks ...

Harkness, Gipton and Braithwaite exit

The Bertrams and their guests have formed into an impromptu house-party choir of voices, humming rather than singing the opening lines of 'Thou Art Gone From My Gaze'

All   Thou are gone from my gaze
                     Like a beautiful dream
                     And I seek thee in vain
                     By the meadow and stream;
                     Oft I breathe thy dear name
                     To the winds floating by
                     But thy sweet voice is mute
                     To my bosom's love sigh ——

The Lights come up on the next scene

SCENE 7

The Drawing-Room, Mansfield Park

Where the assembled voices now begin to softly sing the words of the sixteenth-century ballad

All   In the stillness of night
                     When the stars mildly shine,
                     My heart fondly holds
                     A communion with thine
                     For I feel thou art near
                     And where e'er I may be
                     That thy spirit of love
                     Keeps a watch over me.
                     Thy spirit of love
                     Keeps a watch over me.

As the song ends, the members of the choir hold the close grouped positions, looking out towards the audience, during the following dialogue

Mary Mr Rushworth is looking very happy. November cannot come soon enough. Do you share his eagerness, Miss Bertram?

Maria Yes, Miss Crawford.

Edmund We are all eager for Sir Thomas's safe return, Miss Crawford. That is so.

Mary But it does so put me in mind of those old heathen heroes who offered sacrifices to the gods to celebrate their homecoming.

Edmund There is no sacrifice in this case, Miss Crawford.

Mary I was only joking.

Edmund I have chosen to take holy orders, Miss Crawford, as freely as my sister has chosen matrimony.

Mary I am sure you have. It is fortunate that your inclination and your father's convenience should be so much in accord. I understand that there is a very good living kept for you hereabouts?

Edmund And do you imagine that has influenced my decision?

Fanny I am sure that it has not!

Edmund Thank you, Fanny, for that kind word.

Fanny It is the same thing as for the son of an admiral to go into the navy, or the son of a general to join the army — nobody sees anything wrong in that.

Mary No, Miss Price, and for good reason. The navy and the army are their own justification: heroism, danger, bustle, fashion.

Fanny Miss Crawford ——

Mary It's true. A clergyman has nothing to do but read the newspaper, watch the weather and quarrel with his wife. Never marry a clergyman, Miss Price, or you will be wife to a man whose amiability depends upon his sermons.

Edmund I think the man who could often quarrel with Fanny must be beyond the reach of any sermon.

Mary I fancy Miss Price has been more used to deserve praise, Mr Bertram, than to hear it.

Braithwaite enters

Braithwaite Fanny, embarrassed by the compliment, crossed to look out of the window.

As Fanny crosses downstage to look out of an invisible window, Edmund follows her. The remaining members of the choir again begin to hum the opening lines of the song, softly, as the dialogue continues

Edmund Quite a remarkable person. It is pure joy to listen to her reason! And how easily she joins in with anything and everything. Don't you find her quite remarkable, Fanny?

Fanny Quite. I wish that I had her enthusiasm — except that I think that I prefer it here — looking out into the night. So calm. So quiet. A full moon and not a single cloud in the sky. I sometimes wish I was a poet.

Edmund I like your enthusiasm, Fanny. And I pity all of those that do not share it.

Fanny It was you that taught me to admire the night sky, Edmund.

Edmund And I could not have asked for a better pupil. See — there's Arcturus, looking very bright.

Fanny And there's the Great Bear. I wish I could see Cassiopeia.

Edmund Cassiopeia is at our backs. We must go out on to the lawn to see Cassiopeia tonight. Should you be afraid, Fanny?

Fanny Not in the least. It is a great while since you and I did any star-gazing.
Edmund I cannot, for the life of me, imagine why that should be so ...

*Fanny turns to go outside, but as Edmund moves to go with her, Mary
Crawford begins to sing the words of the song while the others continue to
hum, softly*

We will stay until she has finished, Fanny, and then slip outdoors. (*He
moves back to listen to Mary's solo*)
Braithwaite Fanny, realizing that she had been abandoned yet again, turned
her attention back to the night sky.
Mary   In the stillness of night
                     When the stars mildly shine,
                     My heart fondly holds
                     A communion with thine
                     For I feel thou art near
                     And where e're I may be
                     That thy spirit of love
                     Keeps a watch over me.

*Edmund leads the applause for Mary's solo, while Mrs Norris moves down
to reprimand Fanny*

Mrs Norris Fanny! Don't stand there by the open window, child. You'll
catch your death of cold. Come and keep your Aunt Bertram company.

*Edmund, Mrs Norris and Fanny rejoin the other members of the choir and
reprise the closing lines of the song*

All   Thy spirit of love
                     Keeps a watch over me.

As the song ends, the Lights fade

During the Black-out, Braithwaite, Lady Bertram, Mary and Henry exit

*The Lights come up immediately on Maria, Julia, Tom, Edmund, Mr
Rushworth, Mr Yates and Fanny, with Mrs Norris seated on the periphery*

Edmund A *play*?
Tom Yes, a play!
Edmund You're proposing to perform a play? I trust not here at Mansfield?
Tom Where else? Mr Yates has kindly agreed to act as manager to our
company.

As the scene continues, Tom and Mr Yates, with the assistance of Harkness, and the stage crew, if necessary, bustle on and off stage, bringing the rostra, supports and curtains and trunk containing properties and assemble the small stage themselves

Mr Yates It was all decided days ago.

Edmund I think this is a terrible idea.

Maria I think this is a wonderful idea.

Edmund And where do you propose to find your theatre?

Tom We do not need a theatre — we shall adapt this room to suit our purpose.

Mr Rushworth Provided we have a curtain. A play is not a play that does not have a curtain.

Mr Yates We shall have a curtain.

Tom We shall have a curtain!

Mr Rushworth And it must go up and down — that is most important. Up and down and not from side to side.

Mr Yates A few yards of red velvet will suffice. With a side wing or two to run up, doors for our entrances and exits, and three or four painted backdrops — that will be quite sufficient.

Edmund This has not been mentioned in my presence.

Julia Only because we knew you'd put your disapproving face on, Edmund.

Edmund What disapproving face?

Julia The very one you've got on now.

Maria I can't think why. Nobody loves to see a play more than you do yourself — or would travel further to see one.

Edmund To see real actors, yes. But I would not walk from this room to the next to view the ham-fisted efforts of those not bred to the trade. You are not serious, Tom, in this insanity?

Tom I was never more so. Why not?

Edmund Why not? Because if Father were here he would disapprove of this mad venture far more strongly than I.

Mr Yates Then if I might venture to say so, Mr Bertram, he would be in a very small minority. Private theatricals are all the fashion.

Julia Besides, Edmund, Father is not here.

Maria Father is in Antigua.

Tom Hurrah!

Edmund (*as the stage and wings begin to take shape*) Nay, sir, let us not do anything by halves! Be done with it — why not have a pit and boxes and a gallery! If we don't outdo Ecclesford, we do nothing.

Tom We fully intend to outdo Ecclesford, Edmund. I have taken on a carpenter with that intention in mind. I have also engaged a painter.

Edmund Two workmen?

Tom (*indicating the work in progress*) To help us construct our stage and scenery ——

As if on cue, there is the sound of hammering off stage

They have been in the house for days.

Mr Rushworth We have also decided on the play. It's to be *Lovers' Vows.*

Edmund *Lovers' Vows?*

Mr Rushworth I'm to be Count Cassel — and I'm to come on in an embroidered suit and a pink satin cloak — and later in the play I'm to have a complete change of dress and appear in a hunting costume.

Edmund *(ignoring this last) Lovers' Vows!*

Mr Yates There is not a play that will suit us better — and it means that the work that I put in at Ecclesford shall not go wasted.

Edmund But what about the women's roles?

Maria I'm to take the part which Lady Ravenshaw was to have done — and Miss Crawford is to be Amelia.

Julia And I am to play all the serving women.

Edmund I should have deemed *Lovers' Vows* the worst title you could have settled on.

Mr Rushworth I come on three times and have two and forty speeches. I have not yet counted the number of lines. I shall hardly recognize myself in an embroidered suit and a pink satin cloak ——

Edmund ignores him, pointedly, and he turns back to the others

Well, I won't — and I can't pretend I will.

Harkness enters

Harkness My apologies if the noise of carpentry has caused any distraction — but a theatrical party cannot be organized without constant recourse to the joinery saw and the continual sound of nails hammering into wood. Gentlemen, your opinions would be much appreciated regarding work in progress, coupled with your expert advice vis-à-vis the stage dimensions.

Tom Mr Yates.

Tom and Mr Yates follow Harkness off stage as Gipton enters, carrying a sewing-box

Gipton I'm all fingers-and-thumbs when it comes to needle and thread — but if somebody hadn't stitched ever so many brass curtain rings on to goodness knows how much red velvet material, there would not have been a theatrical entertainment.

Edmund I must tell you, sister, that I feel that *Lovers' Vows* is a play unfit for private performance.

Maria Then we see things differently, Edmund, for I cannot find anything objectionable in the piece.

Edmund Read the first act aloud, I beg of you, either to your mother or your aunt, and see if they approve of it. I am convinced that Father would not approve. Have you read *Lovers' Vows*, Fanny?

Fanny Not yet.

Maria If I were to turn down the part, Edmund, Julia would certainly take it. Besides, I feel sure that we might examine every play that was ever written and find some excuse for not performing it.

Mrs Norris I am not acquainted with the play, Edmund, but if there is anything objectionable in it, surely it can be easily left out?

Mr Rushworth Be assured, madam, that if one single line — nay, one word — of my forty-two speeches was in any way offensive, I would blot it from my memory. Provided, of course, that I had committed it to memory, which I have not yet had time to do. There are so many.

Tom and Mr Yates return, ushering in Henry and Mary

Tom Here are Henry and Miss Crawford to swell our ranks.

Mary Is it decided yet who is to play Anhalt to my Amelia? To which gentleman among you am I to have the pleasure of making love?

Mr Yates We have not yet decided upon our Anhalt, Miss Crawford.

Mr Rushworth I had my choice of parts, but I thought that I should like to be the Count the best. He is, after all, a titled gentleman.

Mary You chose wisely, Mr Rushworth. Anhalt is a difficult part.

Mr Rushworth The Count has forty-two speeches, Miss Crawford, and a change of costume to attend to. It is no trifle, I assure you.

Mary The fact that we have not yet found an Anhalt comes as no surprise.

Henry Amelia is a daring young lady. Her behaviour may well frighten off all possible suitors.

Tom I would be only too happy to take on the role of Anhalt, Miss Crawford. But I am already playing three parts: Landlord, Cottager and Butler.

Mr Yates (*softly to Tom*) Your brother should take on the role. Do you not think he would?

Tom I should not care to ask him. We'll find an Anhalt.

Mr Yates And what is Fanny going to play?

Tom (*conspiratorially*) Maria, a word.

Mr Yates (*equally conspiratorially*) Maria, a word.

Tom and Mr Yates, beckoning to Maria, take her off stage for a word in private

Mary Edmund, may I ask you for your disinterested opinion?

Edmund My advice, Miss Crawford, is that you change the play.

Mary I should have no objection to that, Mr Bertram — for while I feel myself attracted to the part of Amelia, I do not think that I could do her justice unless I felt some sympathy, at least, for the gentleman acting opposite me. If any part could tempt you to act, Mr Bertram, I suppose it might be Anhalt?

Edmund Why should that be?

Mary Because he is a clergyman. Why else?

Edmund That is the last thing that would tempt me into theatricals.

Mary Might I enquire why?

Edmund I would think that a man who has chosen to enter the church is, perhaps, the last man who should act a clergyman on the stage, Miss Crawford.

At which point, Maria, Tom and Mr Yates return

Maria And I tell you that she will not do it.

Mr Yates There is no harm in asking.

Tom Leave it to me. Fanny! You are chosen! You're picked to play Cottager's Wife.

Fanny Oh no, cousin! I could not act in a play to save my life. You must excuse me.

Tom We certainly shall not excuse you. Cottager's Wife is nothing to take fear at. Half a dozen lines to speak at most.

Fanny Edmund, I could not say them. My mouth would open and close and nothing would come out. That would not be acting Cottager's Wife — that would be acting Fanny Price.

Tom It will make no matter if you are not heard, Fanny. The part is unimportant.

Mr Rushworth Heavens! If you are afraid of half a dozen lines, Miss Price, what would you do with a role like mine? I have forty-two entire speeches!

Tom I shall be with you. I am Cottager. I'm your husband. I'll give you a push or a nudge when you need to move.

Fanny Please, Mr Bertram, do not ask it of me. I should only disappoint you.

Tom It has been decided, Fanny. You must find your costume: a brown gown, a white apron.

Mr Yates A mob cap. (*He finds such a cap in a property trunk. He puts the cap on Fanny's head*)

Tom We shall give you a few wrinkles.

Mr Yates A little crowsfoot at the corner of the eyes.

Tom If you stoop a little — so — you'll make an excellent old woman.

Fanny You must excuse me. Please!

Julia Don't be such a creep-mouse, Fanny.

Henry I'm sure you'll do it very well.

Mr Yates You will play the part, Miss Price, as admirably as you are suited
to it.

Mrs Norris What a piece of work is here about nothing! I am ashamed of
you, Fanny, to disoblige your cousins so — considering how kind they are
to you. Take the part with a good grace and let us hear no more
complaining.

Edmund Do not urge her, ma'am. Let her choose for herself. If she does not
wish to act she should not be forced.

Mrs Norris I am not going to force her. But I shall think her a very obstinate,
ungrateful girl, if she does not do as her aunt and cousins wish her. A very
ungrateful girl indeed — considering who and what she is!

Fanny (*rushing from the room, close to tears*) Excuse me, please.

Fanny exits

Mr Rushworth Heavens above! If she had one half — nay, only a quarter
as many words as I have to commit to memory, she might have cause for
anguish.

*Edmund, angry at this lack of feeling, slams downs his playbook and
hastens after Fanny*

*By this point the small stage is constructed, complete with working front
curtain, and with chairs and benches arranged in front, so that the drawing-
room now represents a little theatre. The Lights fade*

*Everyone exits. Braithwaite enters in a spot. During the following, Fanny
enters and the Lights come up to reveal her alone, reading a book*

Braithwaite During a break in the proceedings, when the actors were
distributed in other rooms around the house, in order to learn their lines or
rehearse their separate scenes in private, Fanny took advantage of the quiet
in the drawing-room and tried to lose herself in a learned work concerning
Lord Macartney's travels in the Orient.

Edmund enters. Braithwaite exits

Edmund May I speak to you, Fanny?

Fanny Certainly.

Edmund You will be pleased to hear that it has been decided to ask Mrs
Grant to take on Cottager's Wife. Thankfully, you should be excused.

Fanny I am grateful.

Edmund Also, I should like your opinion.

Fanny *My* opinion?

Edmund You may have been excused, but these theatricals get worse and worse. First, they have chosen a play which I believe to be entirely unsuitable — and now, as if that first circumstance were not bad enough, they are proposing to recruit, for the role of Anhalt, a young man who is hardly known to any of us.

Fanny Oh?

Edmund I have nothing against Charles Maddox as a person ——

Fanny Nor I — nothing at all.

Edmund And yet the thought of him being allowed to act the part of Anhalt to Miss Crawford's Amelia seems highly objectionable to say the least. Do you not agree?

Fanny If it is agreed upon already, there is nothing that can be done.

Edmund There is one thing that can be done, Fanny, and I have decided to do it. I must play Anhalt myself.

Fanny But you are totally opposed to the play!

Edmund Yes — but I can think of no alternative. Can you?

Fanny Not immediately. But surely ——

Edmund But surely? I am surprised that you are not instantly in agreement? Put yourself in Miss Crawford's place, Fanny, if Charles Maddox were to be allowed in. Consider what it would be like for her to have to put her arms around a stranger? Or — what is even worse — for her to suffer a stranger's arm around her waist? Surely her feelings are to be respected?

Fanny I am sorry for Miss Crawford. But I am more sorry, Edmund, to see you drawn into doing something you are totally against. You are giving in to the others.

Edmund I came here to seek your approval, Fanny. I am not comfortable without it.

Fanny Oh, Edmund.

Edmund Without your approval, Fanny, I begin to wonder if I have taken the right decision? I was sure that you would appreciate Miss Crawford's feelings.

Fanny I am sure that she will be pleased. It will come as a great comfort to her, I know, to have you embrace her — and not Mr Maddox ——

Edmund I knew that you would agree with me, but I could not rest assured until I had heard you say so. I shall take great pleasure, tomorrow morning, in strolling down and telling Miss Crawford what I intend to do. I shall leave you to your book. I am sorry to have troubled you with all this acting nonsense — (*he glances at the title of the book which Fanny is holding*) — and leave you to travel back to China, I see, with Lord Macartney.

Edmund exits

The Lights fade, leaving Fanny in a single spot

*Gipton enters, finding her own spot. She carries an ostrich-feather and
needle and thread*

Gipton But the poor girl couldn't concentrate her thoughts on book-reading.
For all Fanny Price cared, China might just as well have been a hundred
miles away! Edmund Bertram had told her the most extraordinary, the
most inconceivable, the most unwelcome news — and she could put her
mind to nothing else ——

Harkness enters attending to a task on the stage

Harkness Edmund Bertram acting on the stage? After all of his objections
to amateur theatricals in general and *Lovers' Vows* in particular? It was all
Miss Crawford's doing.

Braithwaite enters in a spot

Braithwaite Fanny Price had recognized Miss Crawford's influence in every
word that Edmund Bertram had uttered — and she was miserable ——
Gipton It was all misery now ——

The Lights fade up

Fanny closes her book and exits

*Harkness continues to busy himself on stage. Gipton sits down and takes up
needle and thread as she continues*

Mark you, being a housemaid isn't all skylarks neither. There's little time
for snatching sly kisses and quick cuddles with the under-footman — not
if you've been conscripted as a seamstress.
Braithwaite I've been relieved of cleaning grates and laying fires this
morning — first to stitch Lord only knows how many brass curtain rings
on red velvet curtains ——

*She pauses to turn and look at the stage within a stage as Harkness tugs on
a cord, first opening and then closing again, the red velvet curtain*

Harkness That's one job done ——
Gipton And here's another one started. Ooooh! (*She has pricked her thumb
with the needle*) I'm sewing ostrich feathers on floppy hats, would you

believe? (*She holds up the hat containing the feather she has just sewn on*) And what kind of gentleman, might you imagine, would aspire to walking round with that upon his head? One that required his head to be examined, you might beg leave to wonder?

Mr Rushworth enters, wearing a hideous pink cloak

Mr Rushworth Is it ready yet?

Gipton (*to the audience*) You would be right. (*To Mr Rushworth*) As ready as it will ever be.

Mr Rushworth I cannot feel myself inside the part until I feel myself inside the costume. (*He puts on the hat which comes down over his eyes*) How's that?

Gipton and Braithwaite exchange an impish glance and go off giggling. Harkness makes a more dignified exit. During the following, Mary enters. The dialogue, within single quotation marks in the next sequence, is taken from the play "Lovers' Vows", by August von Kotzebue, 1798 (see Production Note on page iv)

It is quite large. Is it too large, I wonder?
　　　'Ah, my dear Colonel! Miss Wildenhaim, I kiss your hand.'
(*He performs an exaggerated bow and the hat falls from his head*) It is too large. Miss Crawford, have you seen Mr Yates, by any happy circumstance?

Mary (*shaking her head*) Have you seen Edmund?

Mr Rushworth (*also shaking his head*) It is imperative that I find him. 'Ah, my dear Colonel!' Those are the words I speak to Baron Wildenhaim, and then I say to you: 'Miss Wildenhaim, I kiss your hand.' (*He repeats his exaggerated bow and, again, his hat falls off*) Do you see the problem?

Mary The hat is much too large for you, Mr Rushworth.

Mr Rushworth Precisely.

Mr Yates enters with Tom, Maria, Henry and Mrs Grant

Mr Yates Good — the carpenters have nearly finished.

Tom They're finishing off the other two backdrops.

Mrs Grant It is a transformation! It is not a drawing-room any longer. It is a real theatre!

Mr Rushworth Mr Yates ——

Mr Yates Not now, Mr Rushworth. Miss Crawford, you should be studying your words with Mr Bertram.

Mary I cannot find him, Mr Yates. I have been looking for him.

Mr Rushworth Mr Yates ——

Mr Yates Later, Mr Rushworth.

Mrs Grant (*discovering the cord which opens and closes the curtains*) It is like a real theatre behind here too. There is a cord to open the curtains and another cord to draw them shut. They are like real theatre curtains.

Mr Rushworth Or would be, Mrs Grant, if they went up and down and not from side to side. Mr Yates ——

Mr Yates In a moment, Mr Rushworth. Would you oblige me, Mrs Grant, by leaving the curtains closed for now? And further oblige me, for the moment, by reading the part of Country Girl?

Mrs Grant I am Cottager's Wife, Mr Yates.

Mr Yates Neither Cottager's Wife nor Country Girl are taxing parts, Mrs Grant. I wondered whether you might consider applying yourself to both?

Mrs Grant I have not learned Cottager's Wife yet, Mr Yates. I would rather sit quietly, somewhere in a corner, and apply myself to that task.

Mr Yates Quietly then.

Mrs Grant I shall be a mouse. But I would rather play one part well than two parts badly.

Mr Rushworth Mr Bertram is playing three parts, Mrs Grant. He is Cottager, Butler and the Landlord. I would take on another role myself, were Count Cassel not such a demanding part with two-and-forty lines, no less. (*He taps his forehead*) They are in here though, every one. Mr Yates ——

Mr Yates A little later, Mr Rushworth. Tom, Maria — Act One, Scene One, A High Road. The Landlord and Agatha Friburg.

As the rehearsals commence, Mrs Grant sits studying her words assiduously, covering her eyes with one hand while mouthing them elaborately but in silence. Mr Rushworth meanwhile struts around rehearsing his part, with particular application to the moment when he parts company with his hat, also in silence

Tom Do you wish us to be on the stage when the curtain opens? Or should we be off the stage and enter?

Mr Yates You should be in the wings, as it stipulates in the book: "The Landlord of the inn leads Agatha by the hand out of the house".

Tom From here?

Mr Yates Yes, yes — from there will suit very well.

Tom "enters" with Maria

Tom 'No, no! No room for you any longer. It is the fair today in the next village. The country people with their wives and children take up every corner I have.'

Maria (*haughtily*) 'You will turn a poor sick woman out of doors who has spent her last farthing in your house?'

Mr Yates Miss Bertram?

Maria Yes?

Mr Yates Not quite so haughty, I think.

Maria Was I haughty? I did not intend it.

Mr Yates You are a poor sick woman who has spent her last farthing. A poor sick woman without so much as a farthing would not be at all haughty — (*He has been trying to ignore Mr Rushworth's posturings but can do so no longer*) Mr Rushworth? Mr Rushworth!

Mr Rushworth Ah! Mr Yates! You are ready for me now?

Mr Yates No, sir, I am not. Can you not find another place to practise Count Cassel?

Mr Rushworth (*a gust of petulant anger*) Willingly, Mr Yates! I will go out into the grounds and be him — if you will spare me a moment first! (*Calmer*) I have this problem. When I come out on to the stage, my first words are to Baron Wildenhaim, yourself. I say to him: 'Ah, my dear Colonel!' And then I turn to Amelia, his daughter, which is Miss Crawford, and I say ... and I say ... What do I say?

Mary You say 'Miss Wildenhaim, I kiss your hand.'

Mr Rushworth 'Miss Wildenhaim, I kiss your hand.' (*He does his usual bow and, as always, his hat falls off*) You see the problem, Mr Yates? It is too large for me.

Mr Yates In the presence of a lady, surely you would remove your hat before presenting your compliments?

Mr Rushworth digests this information slowly

Mr Rushworth Of course. Of course! The problem is solved! Mr Yates, you are a genius.

Mr Rushworth claps Mr Yates' theatrical intelligence and the rest of the cast of Lovers' Vows joins in. Mr Yates accepts these plaudits modestly, but his enjoyment is spoiled by another burst of hammering from off stage

Mr Yates God give me ... Stop that confounded clatter. What is that noise?

Tom It is the carpenter, Mr Yates.

Mr Yates Who's there?

A workman enters

Who are you?

Workman Carpenter, sir.

Mr Yates I said "who" not "what". I want your name, carpenter, not your occupation.

Workman That is my name. Carpenter. Thomas Carpenter. I am the scene painter.

More offstage hammering

That is the carpenter.

Mr Yates Follow me, actors. We shall rehearse our piece in the billiard-room — away from this confounded clatter.

Everyone, except Mary, exits. Braithwaite enters, followed by Fanny

Braithwaite Exit Mr Yates and his cast, with the exception of Mary Crawford. Fanny enters and, unaware of Mary's presence, thinking the room empty, she steps on to the stage and allows herself a few theatrical gestures and curtsies.

Mary Very prettily done, Miss Price.

Fanny (*embarrassed*) Miss Crawford ——

Mary They are all gone somewhere else.

Fanny I was not looking for anyone. I had put a book down somewhere. Perhaps I left it in the library.

Mary I should not venture into any room, Miss Price. You may stumble upon my brother and Miss Bertram practising at being Frederick and Agatha. It might not be wise to interrupt them.

Fanny Perhaps it is in my own room.

Mary I would not consider anywhere entirely safe. Except in here. Don't go, Miss Price. I was looking for somewhere to practise my Amelia alone. I wonder if I might impose on your kindness and ask you to listen to me.

Fanny If it would help to have me hear your words, Miss Crawford, I could hardly refuse.

Mary I do not think that I could go through them with Edmund until I have found some courage. I did not think much of it at first, but upon my word, there really is a speech or two that ... (*She shows Fanny a page in her playbook*) There, look at that speech, and that — and there again. How am I to look Edmund in the face and say such things? Could you do it? But then, he is your cousin, which makes all the difference. Will you rehearse it with me, so that I may pretend that you are he, and take it speech by speech? You have a look of him sometimes.

Fanny (*flattered*) Have I? I will do the best I can, Miss Crawford.

Mary Will you listen to my soliloquy? It is in Act Three. (*She gives her book to Fanny, indicating the page and place, then crosses on to the stage*) 'It is my father's will that I should marry — it is my father's wish to see me happy —' Yes?

Fanny 'If then, you love me as I say, I will marry; and will be happy — but only with you.'

Mary How prettily you say the words, Miss Price. A pity indeed that you did not yield to your cousin's entreaties and accept a part in our little entertainment. Remind of that speech again.

Fanny Which part of it?

Mary The same part that you spoke before.

Edmund enters, unseen by Fanny

Fanny 'If then, you love me as I say, I will marry; and will be happy, but only with you.'

Fanny breaks off as she realizes that Edmund is there

Mary Edmund, I looked all over the house for you. How clever of you to find me here.

Edmund Particularly so, Miss Crawford, as I was not even looking for you. I have been searching high and low for Fanny.

Fanny For me, Edmund?

Edmund (*displaying his own playbook*) I wondered if you might hear me speak my lines.

Mary We are both of the same mind then, Edmund. Miss Price has been listening to mine.

Edmund Then perhaps, Miss Crawford, we might take advantage of Fanny's presence and prevail upon her good nature not only to hear us both together, but also to act as prompter?

Mary As I have already explained to Miss Price, Mr Bertram, I am not sure that I am ready yet for such a circumstance.

Edmund You are not yet sure of your lines?

Mary Act Two presents no difficulty, Mr Bertram.

Edmund We have no scenes to act together in Act Two.

Mary Precisely. My only scene in Act Two, Miss Price, is with Baron Wildenhaim — which is Mr Yates.

Edmund And are the scenes you have with me the ones with which you are not yet comfortable?

Mary They are the ones that present most problem, Mr Bertram.

Edmund Then we should confront that problem here and now and while we have good opportunity. (*He locates page and place and hands the book to Fanny*) We shall begin here, Fanny, at the end of my long speech where Anhalt cries out: 'Oh, liberty, dear liberty!' And Amelia says ——

Fanny 'I will not marry.'

Mary 'I will not marry.'

Edmund 'You mean to say you will not fall in love.'

Mary 'Oh, no! I am in love.'

Edmund 'You are in love? And with the Count?'
Mary 'I wish I were.'
Edmund 'Why so?'
Mary 'Because he would, perhaps, love me in return.'
Edmund 'Who is there that would not?'
Mary 'Would you?'
Edmund 'I — I — I am your tutor. I am out of the question.'
Mary 'Yes, you have instructed me for a long time now. Perhaps it is time that I began to teach you.'
Edmund 'You — teach?'
Mary 'Why not? Only a woman can teach the science of herself.'
Edmund (*having dried, looking across at Fanny*) Yes, Fanny?

But Fanny's eyes have strayed from the page during the above

Fanny I'm sorry!
Mary From 'Only a woman can teach the science of herself.'
Edmund What do I say next?
Fanny (*still frantically scanning pages*) I'm sorry.
Edmund No matter.
Fanny 'I will not marry.'
Edmund I will not marry?
Mary Anhalt does not say 'I will not marry.' 'I will not marry' is Amelia's line — after Anhalt says 'Oh, liberty, dear liberty.'
Fanny I'm sorry.
Mary It's across the page. After Amelia says: 'Oh, liberty, dear liberty.'
Fanny It's here. I'm sorry. Amelia says: 'Only a woman can teach the science of herself,' and then Anhalt replies: 'I love you more than life — Oh, Amelia ... '
Edmund Of course I do. Shall you repeat the closing words of your previous speech, Miss Crawford, in order that I might fix it in my head?
Fanny 'Only a woman can teach the science of herself.'

Mary gives her a frosty smile

I'm sorry.
Mary 'Only a woman can teach the science of herself.'
Edmund 'I love you more than life. Oh, Amelia, had we lived in those golden times which the poets picture ... But the world is changed — your birth and fortune make our union impossible.'
Mary 'It is my father's wish that I should marry. It is my father's wish to see me happy. If then, you love me as you say, I will marry — and will be happy — but only with you. I will tell him this, and he will say: "If he loves you,

and you love him, in the name of heaven let it be!" Then I shall hug him round the neck, kiss his hands, run away from him and fly to you — and heaven's blessing will surely follow ... '

Gipton enters

Gipton Fanny watched, as though mesmerized, as Mary slipped her arms around Edmund's waist and offered him her mouth.

Before Edmund can take advantage of this offer however:

Julia rushes in

Julia Edmund — Father is home!
Edmund He cannot be.
Julia He is! He is in the hall.

Mr Yates enters

Mr Yates What should we do? What shall you tell him?
Edmund Whoever has arrived, it is not Sir Thomas. He has barely left Antigua. He is somewhere at sea.

Mr Rushworth enters in haste, without his ostrich-feather-trimmed hat but still wearing his garish pink cloak

Mr Rushworth Sir Thomas is back! I was practising my lines down by the lily pond when I heard coach wheels on the drive — and next a servant call: "Sir Thomas is back!"
Mr Yates There will be no play. He will cancel the performance.

Tom enters

Tom You've heard the news?
Mr Yates Upon my word, it will be like Ecclesford all over again.
Edmund Where are Mr Crawford and Maria?
Mary They were rehearsing in the library.
Edmund Miss Crawford, it would be best if you were to find your brother and go home quietly — until we have made our explanations, at least.
Tom Julia, go with her to the library.

Julia and Mary exit

Mr Rushworth Shall I go too? Had I not better go too? Will it not be right for me to go too?

Edmund No, sir — you should stay. But you would be better out of costume.

Mr Rushworth Heavens! Thank heaven he did not see me. Thank heaven I had the foresight to steal away across the lawn and creep in through a side door. (*He starts to bundle up his cloak*)

Sir Thomas enters, carrying the ostrich-feather-trimmed hat

Sir Thomas Can someone tell me what is going on? Tom? Edmund? What is this?

Edmund Father, welcome home.

Tom It is a theatre, Father.

Sir Thomas I can see it is a theatre. I have the wit to recognize a theatre when I see one. Except, when I was last in here it was a drawing-room. What is happening at my house? First I catch sight of some madman capering across the lawn, half-crouched, with this monstrosity upon his head. It fell off as he ran. When I discover its owner, I shall ...

Sir Thomas's glance falls on Mr Rushworth who is trying to conceal the cloak behind his back

Who is this?

Edmund This is Mr Rushworth, sir, who is to marry Maria.

Sir Thomas Have we not met before, Mr Rushworth?

Mr Rushworth No, sir. Never before, sir. No, sir, never.

Tom And this is Mr Yates, sir, who is staying with us having lately been staying with Lord Ravenshaw.

Mr Yates Who instructed me to deliver his best compliments, Sir Thomas.

Tom It was Mr Yates, sir, who was the origin of our acting passion.

Edmund and Mr Rushworth join Tom in pointing accusing fingers at Mr Yates

Mr Yates I fear I brought the infection with me from Ecclesford — and it has spread as fashions always spread.

Tom The faster though, in this instance probably, from your having so encouraged in us a love of theatre.

Sir Thomas A love for the theatre in its proper place, sir, inside a proper theatre — and not inside one's home.

Edmund We have all of us been more or less to blame, sir, everyone excepting Fanny. Her feelings have been against the venture from first to last.

Fanny has been hanging back, shyly, but Sir Thomas beckons her forward

Sir Thomas Fanny! Dear little Fanny. (*He kisses her affectionately*) How
pretty you have grown.
Mr Yates We beseech your indulgence, Sir Thomas. As young performers
we beseech your indulgence.
Sir Thomas It is given. I am come home to be happy and indulgent. Let us
summon all of the family together. But I think that we shall put an end of
these home-grown theatricals.

As they all move off in one direction, Harkness enters from another

Harkness Sir Thomas is a gentleman who suits words with deeds. The
scene-painter has been dismissed already—having been here long enough
to spoil the floor of one room, ruin all the coachman's sponges and make
five under-servants idle and dissatisfied. And I have to now pull down that
on which several days were spent in putting up. But not yet awhile ...

Harkness moves out of sight as Maria and Henry enter

Maria You must go, Mr Crawford. Mr Crawford, you must.
Henry A minute longer.
Maria Your sister will be halfway home by now — and Mr Rushworth will
be wondering where I am at. Or, worse still, with whom.
Henry One last look at our little theatre, Miss Bertram, before it is taken
down. A pity. I was looking forward to my theatrical début at Mansfield
Park. I have a penchant for the profession. I really believe I could be fool
enough to take on any character that was ever written. (*He springs up on
to the stage and proceeds to impress Maria with his acting abilities*) "My
liege, I did deny no prisoners. But I remember when the fight was done,
when I was dry with rage and extreme toil, breathless and faint, leaning
upon my sword!"

Maria applauds and he is encouraged to continue

"My horse, my horse, my kingdom for a horse!"

More applause

"Hath not a Jew eyes? Hath not a Jew hands, organs, dimensions, senses,
affections, passions? Fed by the same food, hurt with the same weapons,
subject to the same diseases, healed by the same means, warmed and
cooled by the same winter and summer as a Christian is?"

More applause

I am also equal to comedy. "I grant you, friends, if that should fright the ladies out of their wits, they would have no more discretion but to hang us; but I will aggravate my voice so that I will roar you as gently as any sucking dove; I will roar you as t'were any nightgale."
Maria You have not been truthful with us, Mr Crawford. You have been in theatricals before. How sad that we are to be denied your Frederick.
Henry Ah! And with you as Agatha, Miss Bertram, how could I have failed? No man could wish for a prettier mother.

Maria has joined Henry on the stage

'Why should I wish to know my father if you tell me he is a villain. My heart is satisfied with a mother. I will work all day at the plough and all night with my pen. It will do, Mother, it will do! Heaven's goodness will assist me — it will prosper the endeavours of a dutiful son for the sake of a helpless mother. I will carry you in my arms to Alsace.'
Maria 'What mother could seek a finer son?'

Maria takes Henry in her arms and he embraces her in return, allowing one of his hands to steal up and gently knead her breast

Mr Crawford — no! This is not the manner of mother and son.
Henry But we are not Frederick and Agatha, Miss Bertram. Sir Thomas has returned, remember. He has put an end to play-acting.
Maria Goodbye to *Lovers' Vows* then.
Henry Goodbye to *Lovers' Vows*.

Henry presses his mouth on Maria's and after a pretence at struggle, she kisses him back, hungrily

Harkness enters from out of the shadows and tugs at the cord, drawing the curtain on them

Harkness When real life takes over from pretence upon a stage, it is time to draw the curtain.

CURTAIN

ACT II

SCENE 1

The Drawing-Room, Mansfield Park

Where Lady Bertram, holding her pug dog on her lap, is sitting next to Mrs Norris on the chaise-longue, *with Fanny in attendance and Sir Thomas also standing close at hand. Tom, Edmund, Mr Yates, Mr Rushworth, Julia and Maria are also present. Maria looks despondent*

Harkness enters

During the following, Tom and Edmund move, in turn, and add their own copies of the Lovers' Vows *playbooks to the small stack of similar volumes which have been deposited* C

Harkness How unfortunate it is when a theatrical enterprise of such great pitch and monument, backed by immense enthusiasm, comes to nothing. And how wretched, how unpardonable, how hopeless and how wicked it is to marry without affection. But such a fate, I fear, would seem to be the lot of Miss Maria Bertram.

Harkness moves and picks up the stack of playbooks

Sir Thomas Harkness!
Harkness Yes, Sir Thomas?
Sir Thomas Are those the copies of the play that I instructed you to collect together?
Harkness They are, Sir Thomas.
Sir Thomas You have scoured every room in the house? You have found them all?
Harkness Every single one, Sir Thomas.

Lady Bertram holds up a copy which has been hidden at her side

Lady Bertram Not quite.
Harkness My apologies, your ladyship.

Harkness moves to collect the final playbook as Mr Rushworth seeks to ingratiate himself with Sir Thomas

Mr Rushworth Speaking personally, I must say that I am pleased that we have put the play-acting behind us.
Sir Thomas I am glad to hear it, Mr Rushworth.
Mr Rushworth In my opinion, it is very disagreeable to be continually rehearsing. Did I tell you, sir, that I had two-and-forty entire speeches to commit to memory?
Sir Thomas You may have mentioned it, in passing.
Mr Rushworth I cannot conjecture how I might have managed such a monumental task.
Mrs Norris You have read it, sister?
Lady Bertram I have tried.
Mrs Norris How very courageous of you.
Lady Bertram I got no further than the first few pages, alas, before I was forced to set it aside.
Mrs Norris Is it so offensive, sister?
Lady Bertram That is something I was never to discover. It was fatigue and fatigue alone that caused me to put it down. The concentration that reading requires is quite simply too much for me. Fanny, dear?
Fanny Yes, Aunt?
Lady Bertram Summon me a servant.

Harkness starts to exit with his stack of playbooks

Harkness (*pausing*) I shall consign these to the gardener's bonfire, in accordance with Sir Thomas's instructions — and all trace of the theatrical misadventure will have been erased. The drawing-room is back to being a drawing-room; the red velvet curtain has been taken by Mrs Norris, who has a particular need for red velvet in her cottage.

Harkness exits. Gipton enters

Gipton And I am better suited back at her ladyship's beck and call than I was at stitching ostrich feathers on ill-fitting hats ... You summoned me, your ladyship?
Lady Bertram Plump me a cushion, Gipton.
Gipton (*to the audience*) Well, why not? Plumping cushions is certainly better than sewing hats for Mr Rushworth, or red velvet curtains for Mrs Norris's cottage. (*She plumps a cushion and puts it behind Lady Bertram's back as she looks across at the despondent Maria*) It's Miss Bertram I am

most sorry for. She is still meant to marry Mr Rushworth — and even Sir Thomas is beginning to wonder what sort of son-in-law he has been sentenced to be saddled with ...

Mr Rushworth If I must say as I think, it is not only the acting that is at fault — it is who one is required to do one's acting with. Sir Thomas, you have not yet met Mr Henry Crawford?

Sir Thomas No, and I would value your opinion.

Mr Rushworth I do not say he is not gentleman-like, considering — but it is as well you are aware before you do meet him: he is hardly five foot eight in stature.

Sir Thomas Is he not, Mr Rushworth?

Mr Rushworth Frankly, Sir Thomas, it would not surprise me to discover that he was little more than five foot seven and a half inches.

Sir Thomas I am much obliged to you, Mr Rushworth, for that valuable information.

Braithwaite enters

Gipton Miss Bertram has been hoping against hope to be saved from such a marriage by the intervention of Mr Crawford.

Braithwaite But there has been neither sight nor sound of that gentleman since the night of their encounter in the drawing-room.

Gipton Nor is he likely to put in an appearance neither, if you ask my opinion ——

Harkness enters

Harkness Mr Henry Crawford has called.

During the following, Henry Crawford enters and is taken over to Sir Thomas

Braithwaite Which goes to show how highly one person's opinion may be valued. Miss Bertram watched with both delight and agitation as the man with whom she was so desperately in love was introduced to her father by Mrs Norris. Hope rose in her breast that he had come to request her hand in marriage.

Gipton, Braithwaite and Harkness exit

Sir Thomas I am pleased to have met you, sir.

Henry As I am equally delighted to have made your acquaintance at last, Sir Thomas. Lady Bertram. A delight, sir, that is tempered with sadness in the knowledge that our first encounter must be brief.

Sir Thomas You cannot stay?

Henry No more than a moment. I have a carriage waiting.

Tom Mr Crawford, I was not aware that you were going away? I shall be sad to see you go.

Henry This very day — and I shall be gone for several weeks. I am to meet my uncle first at Bath. But if the play is to be revived — *Lovers' Vows* — it is the one thing that could instantly bring me back from any place in England at an hour's notice.

Tom As to the play, that is entirely at an end.

Edmund It is early for Bath, Mr Crawford. You will find hardly anyone there.

Henry My uncle is always one of the first arrivals. If you will excuse me — I hope to get as far as Banbury today.

Tom I will come with you as far as your carriage. I had intended going for a walk.

Henry (*turning, at last, towards Maria*) Miss Bertram.

Maria Mr Crawford.

Henry I would expect to be back at Mansfield in time to be present at your marriage to Mr Rushworth, but in the unlikely event that I am not, may I now extend my very best heartfelt wishes for your future in that union?

Maria Thank you, Mr Crawford. I am pleased to accept them.

Henry A great shame that *Lovers' Vows* is not to see the light of day; I enjoyed practising our play-acting together enormously.

Maria You certainly seemed to possess a talent for it, Mr Crawford — at times, I might almost have believed that we were not play-acting at all.

Henry proffers Maria his hand and she takes it

Henry Goodbye then.

Maria A safe journey, Mr Crawford.

Gipton enters

Gipton Exit Henry Crawford followed by Tom Bertram. Sir Thomas made it clear to the others that he wished to speak to his daughter, Maria, alone.

Sir Thomas crosses to a prominent position and clears his throat, importantly

Taking the hint, everyone leaves Maria and Sir Thomas alone

They sit on the chaise-longue

Sir Thomas Maria?

Maria Father?

Sir Thomas Are you happy, Maria?

Maria Do I not appear so?

Sir Thomas Sometimes — and sometimes you appear to be the opposite of happy.

Maria I am shortly to be married, sir. And to the gentleman I have freely chosen. A gentleman both of substance and of property. The more time I spend in Mr Rushworth's company, the more I come to realize that he is kind and he is considerate. How could I be less than happy?

Sir Thomas If you tell me so, my dear.

Maria I am happy.

Sir Thomas I only wish you to be aware, Maria, that if at any time you should harbour so much as the slightest doubt with regard to the prospect of this marriage — no matter what inconvenience may have to be faced — you should turn your back on it.

Maria Why should I choose to do that, sir, when I am completely happy?

Sir Thomas (*shaking his head*) And I would also wish you to be assured that, should you come to that decision, you may count upon me, as your father, to act on your behalf and see to it that you are released from this engagement.

Maria Thank you for that, sir. But you are quite mistaken in supposing that I now have — or ever shall have — the smallest desire for breaking my engagement to Mr Rushworth. I am happy.

Sir Thomas Then having been given that assurance, Maria, I can only wish you well in marriage — and am glad to share your happiness with you.

Sir Thomas and Maria exit

The Lights dim and come up again

Gipton enters, carrying a bridal gown

Gipton But Miss Bertram was by no means happy. I am back at work with the pins and needles: but sewing lovers' knots on gowns is a far more pleasurable occupation than sewing Lord-knows-how-many brass rings on red velvet curtains for *Lovers' Vows*.

Maria enters

Maria Is that my wedding gown arrived for a first fitting?

Gipton Coming, Miss Bertram. Miss Bertram's happiness has been destroyed by Henry Crawford. But she has sworn to herself that she will never let him see that he has done it ——

Gipton goes off with Maria as Braithwaite enters

Braithwaite She must escape from Mansfield Park as soon as marriage will allow — and find consolation for her wounded spirit in fortune and consequence, in bustle and the world ——

Braithwaite exits and Harkness enters, carrying the bridegroom's wedding suit

Harkness To such feelings, delay, even the delay of much preparation, would be an evil to Miss Bertram — and as for Mr Rushworth, why, he could hardly be more impatient for the marriage than Miss Bertram is herself.

Mr Rushworth enters

Mr Rushworth Is that my tailor come at last with the suit I am to be married in?
Harkness It is indeed, sir!

Mr Rushworth takes the suit and bustles off

The two principals, being all agreed in this respect, it soon became clear that a few short weeks would be sufficient for such arrangements as must precede the wedding ceremony.

As Harkness exits, the Lights dim and come up again on Fanny, sitting on the chaise-longue *reading a book and with a glass of wine at her side. Edmund enters and sits beside her*

Edmund You will have more time than ever, Fanny, for quiet reflection, when Maria has gone off to be Mrs Rushworth.
Fanny But I prefer Mansfield when it is quiet, Edmund. I am happy sitting by the fire on these autumn evenings with a glass of wine, listening to my uncle talk of the East Indies. I could listen to him for an hour together. It entertains me more than other things have done. But then, I am unlike other people, I dare say.
Edmund Why should you dare say that? Are you chasing compliments?
Fanny No, Edmund ——
Edmund Go to my father if it is compliments you seek, Fanny. But he will not compliment your mind, so much as he will compliment your looks.
Fanny (*embarrassed*) Edmund, you mustn't talk so!

Edmund Why shouldn't he admire you? If you cannot bear an uncle's
admiration, Fanny, what is to become of you? You must try not to mind
growing up into a pretty woman.

Fanny Don't talk so, Edmund! Don't talk so!

Edmund My father is most pleased at the change he sees in you, Fanny —
except, perhaps, in one respect.

Fanny Oh?

Edmund I think it would please him even more if you would talk sometimes,
instead of only listen.

Fanny But I do talk to him more than I did before. I am sure I do. At least,
I try to.

Edmund Miss Crawford was right in what she said about you the other day.

Fanny You have discussed me, Edmund, with Miss Crawford?

Edmund Discussed is hardly the word for it, Fanny. You were hardly the
subject of a serious conversation.

Fanny Oh?

Edmund She did no more than mention her opinion of you, in passing.

Fanny And am I to be allowed to hear Miss Crawford's opinion of me —
in passing?

Edmund Why not? She is a most remarkable young woman. She said that
you seem to be as afraid of being noticed as other women fear being
ignored.

Fanny I see.

Edmund She is such an excellent judge of character. I sometimes think,
Fanny, that Miss Crawford knows you better than you know yourself.

Fanny Perhaps she does.

Edmund I wonder what she thinks of Father? She is such a conversationalist,
I know that they could become the best of friends. If anything, it is his
reserve that prevents it. I hope she does not think that he dislikes her.

Gipton enters

Gipton Begging your pardon, Miss Price, but her ladyship has put something
down somewhere and is most concerned that you are not about to pick it up.

Fanny Thank you, Gipton. I do not think, Edmund, that you need concern
yourself on Miss Crawford's account. As you say yourself, she is such an
excellent judge of character — I am sure that she will have judged her own
well enough to know that she is liked by everyone. Excuse me ...

Fanny hastens off

*Edmund is left to puzzle over her last remark, as the Lights dim, leaving
Gipton in a spot*

Edmund exits

Gipton She could have said a great deal more, but it seemed safer to say nothing, and leave untouched all of Miss Crawford's talents, her accomplishments, her spirits and her importance, lest it might betray Miss Price into observations that might appear ungracious. Besides, there were more important matters close at hand ...

Gipton exits

SCENE 2

The Chapel, Mansfield Park

Harkness is in a spot

During the following, the Lights come up on Dr Grant, Mr Rushworth and Maria, with Tom standing next to the groom and Sir Thomas next to the bride

Harkness It was a very proper wedding. The bride was elegantly dressed. The two bridesmaids were duly inferior. Her father gave her away. Her mother stood with salts in hand expecting to be agitated. Her brother, Tom, was best man. Her Aunt Norris tried to cry. And the service was impressively read by Doctor Grant.

Dr Grant begins the service with his back to the audience, but turns to thunder out his words downstage as he relishes their implications

Dr Grant Dearly beloved, we are gathered together here in the sight of God, and in the face of this congregation, to join together this Man and this Woman in holy matrimony; which is an honourable estate, instituted of God in the time of man's innocence, signifying unto us the mystical union that is betwixt Christ and his Church; and therefore is not by any to be enterprised, nor taken in hand unadvisedly, lightly, or wantonly, to satisfy men's carnal lusts and appetites, like brute beasts that have no understanding; but reverently, discreetly, advisedly, soberly, and in the fear of God; duly considering the causes for which Man was ordained.

Dr Grant turns back to face the bride and groom and pauses while Tom locates the ring in an inside pocket and places it on the open prayer-book. Dr Grant proffers the prayer-book to Mr Rushworth who takes the ring and places it on Maria's finger

Almighty God, who at the beginning did create our first parents, Adam and Eve, and did sanctify and join them together in marriage, pour upon you the riches of his grace, sanctify and bless you, that ye may please him both in body and soul, and live together in holy love unto your lives' end. Amen.

All Amen.

Mr Rushworth kisses Maria clumsily then takes her arm and leads her off, followed by Sir Thomas and Tom, with Dr Grant bringing up the rear. At the same time, Henry enters from one direction and Mary from another. During the following, Fanny enters

Mary You were delayed, Henry?

Henry Twice — once in leaving Newark and then again when one of the horses cast a shoe. It is of no great consequence.

Mary None at all, I should have thought. Why hurry back in time to kiss a bride that you have kissed sufficiently, and often enough, before? But if you were hoping, Henry, that with one Bertram sister married off, you might now turn your attention to the other Bertram sister — you are unlucky on that count also. Julia is invited on the holiday.

Henry Then I must needs look elsewhere for amusement.

Fanny wanders around the stage, lost in happy thought, without once glancing over at the Crawfords. Henry, meanwhile, cannot take his eyes off Fanny

Mary Not, I trust, towards Fanny Price?

Henry Fanny Price — I mean to make her fall in love with me.

Mary Miss Fanny Price?

Henry Why not?

Mary Fanny Price! She's a mouse.

Henry Because you have been here and seen her almost every day, you have not noticed the change in her. She is a different creature to the Fanny Price that was here at Mansfield when I went away.

Fanny exits

Mary How is she different?

Henry She has grown up.

Mary She has always been pretty, Henry — but never strikingly. She is no beauty. She's "pretty enough", as people say. She is just what she was before.

Henry There is more than prettiness to Fanny Price, Mary, and I intend to discover what it is. Her eyes say "I will not like you — I am determined not to like you," and I say that she shall.

Mary Don't make her unhappy, Henry. She feels things deeply,

Henry Haven't I told you? I intend to make her love me. Where's the unhappiness in that? I only want for her to look upon me kindly; to give me smiles as well as blushes; to keep a chair for me by her side, wherever we may be, and to show delight whenever I choose to sit beside her; to be interested in myself and me alone and only me — and to want to keep me here at Mansfield longer than I intend to stay.

Mary Is that all?

Henry One thing more. After I am gone, she must feel that she shall never be happy again.

Mary Moderation itself! And how long do you intend to stay here this time?

Henry Two weeks at the very least — possibly three.

Mary I wish you every success, Henry. But I cannot think that you will have opportunity in the time at your disposal.

Mary exits

Henry (*calling after her*) In matters of the heart, Mary, there is always opportunity — or one makes opportunity for oneself.

Henry exits, and the Lights dim. Gipton enters in a spot, carrying a letter

Gipton But opportunity was to present itself the very next day. And not once — but twice. Firstly, in the shape of a letter which arrived from Portsmouth. Miss Price! Miss Price!

The Lights come up on a bare stage

Fanny enters, takes the letter and opens it eagerly, while Harkness enters from another direction, carrying a newspaper

Harkness And, secondly, in the printed columns of the daily newspaper, Henry Crawford came across an item which would give him cause to visit Mansfield Park.

Henry enters, takes the newspaper from Harkness, discovers an item in its pages, then moves to where Fanny is reading her letter

Henry Miss Price?

Fanny Mr Crawford?

Henry I came as quickly as I could. There is a paragraph in today's *Times* that I felt sure would be of interest to you: "His Majesty's battleship, *The Antwerp*, is returned from the Mediterranean and has anchored at Portsmouth." Is not that the vessel your brother is midshipman aboard?

Fanny Thank you for the thought, Mr Crawford — but I fear that you have had a wasted walk. I have had that news already. William had written to me as soon as his ship had come into port. What's more, he set off himself from Portsmouth early yesterday to come and visit ...

Fanny breaks off as Midshipman William Price, RN, twenty years old, enters, followed by Harkness, carrying a seaman's chest

William! My dearest William!
William Fanny! Little Fanny!

Braithwaite enters

Braithwaite They embraced, once, then stood apart at arm's length and held hands whilst they examined each other's faces — and then they embraced again and with a depth of emotion such as Henry had not seen from her before ——

During the following, the Lights fade, leaving the two Servants in spots

As Harkness speaks, Fanny and William exit, hand-in-hand. Henry follows them

Harkness And, in that moment, Fanny's attractions increased two-fold, for he was no longer in doubt as to the capabilities of her heart. It would be something, he told himself, to be loved by such a girl — to excite the first ardours of her young, unsophisticated mind. She became more desirable to him than she had ever been before. Neither a fortnight, nor three weeks even, would be long enough, he decided.
Braithwaite What was more, it had occurred to him that the midshipman's presence might provide him with the best opportunity of all to find favour with Fanny Price.

Scene 3

The Drawing-Room, Mansfield Park

This now contains two tables, both covered with green baize material, in preparation for a card game

Lady Bertram, Mrs Norris, Mrs Grant and Mary Crawford are seated around one table; Edmund, Dr Grant, Henry and Sir Thomas are at the other, with Fanny standing. All of them are listening to William who holds c

William The cannon-ball struck clean through the long-boat's bows, taking off the bosun's foot, and the boat went down beneath us in a matter of seconds.

Sir Thomas And after you were sunk, young man, how long were you left to struggle in the water?

William As long as the battle raged, sir. An hour at least.

Mrs Grant And the gentleman that lost his foot? Was he also in the sea for a whole hour?

William He did not survive, ma'am.

Lady Bertram How very disagreeable. I wonder anybody can ever go to sea.

William I managed well enough on some floating wreckage. Being the Mediterranean, the water was warm. I suffered no great hardship.

Henry All the same, it is an exciting tale, and told exceedingly well.

Henry applauds and the rest follow his lead

Mrs Norris Where are the playing cards? Sir Thomas, I understood that the girl had been despatched, some minutes since, to fetch playing cards?

Sir Thomas And so she was.

Gipton enters, carrying a tray containing the cards, etc.

Gipton And so she was — and so she has — along with the pencils from the schoolroom for setting down the scores, the paper from the writing room. I have almost had to tour the house and she wonders why it takes so long.

Gipton crosses and unloads playing cards, etc., at one table, unnoticed by Mrs Norris, sitting at the other table

Mrs Norris If they are not here shortly, we must forego all thought of playing cards — the carriage will be waiting for our guests.

Gipton (*putting down the cards, etc., at Mrs Norris's table*) Playing Whist is all well and good — but it might be more beneficial if someone were to teach Mrs Norris Patience.

Gipton flounces out

Lady Bertram Sir Thomas, are we to play Whist or Speculation? Which will amuse me most?

Sir Thomas Speculation, I should think. It is so much more diverting and much less demanding.

Lady Bertram Speculation then. Fanny! I don't know how to play the game, but Fanny shall teach me.

Braithwaite enters

Braithwaite Fanny crossed to the other table, casting backward glances at both William and Edmund whose company she was loathe to leave.
Fanny I have never learned Speculation myself, Aunt Bertram.

Mary stands up and, during the following, moves to watch at Sir Thomas's table

Lady Bertram (*patting the chair which Mary has vacated*) Sit down, niece, and we shall pool our ignorance.
Dr Grant It is quite easily picked up.
Henry (*crossing to the other table*) If I may be allowed to stand between yourself and Miss Price, your ladyship, I would be delighted to assist you both.
Lady Bertram Shall you take first turn at dealing, Mrs Grant? I find that shuffling cards cramps my fingers.
Braithwaite Conversation lapsed at the card-table as Mrs Grant dealt slowly and inexpertly then, across the room:
Dr Grant Is there any word on your eldest son, Sir Thomas?
Sir Thomas Apart from the fact that he is in London, and with that theatrical fellow ——
Lady Bertram Mr Yates, dear.
Sir Thomas —— Mr Yates —— not a word.
Mrs Grant Is it five cards or six each for Speculation, I can never seem to remember?
Mrs Norris Seven.

Braithwaite exits

Mary I understand, Mr Bertram, that you are to take up residence shortly at Thornton Lacey?
Edmund As soon as I have been ordained, Miss Crawford. In three months time. Thornton Lacey is to become my living.
Mary Then you should ask my brother to assist you with any improvements that may need doing to the grounds. You would be willing to assist Edmund with the gardens at his parsonage, wouldn't you, Henry?
Henry I should be more than pleased to do so. I chanced to pass through Thornton Lacey, after the hunt, only last week —— my horse had taken lame and I was forced to walk home. I passed by the parsonage. You will need a new garden at the back of the house ... Excuse me, your ladyship, but you must always follow suit —— the suit is hearts.
Lady Bertram Ah, hearts ... (*Then, discovering that she can follow suit, does so, as the game continues*) Hearts!

Henry (*back to Edmund*) And something needs to be done with the stream, I am not sure what — but I have two or three thoughts up my sleeve that you might care to consider.

William moves across to watch the game in progress at Sir Thomas's table

Edmund I am obliged to you, Mr Crawford. (*He lays down his cards*)
Sir Thomas We'll count you out of this hand, shall we, Edmund?
Edmund (*to Mary*) I am in no position, financially, to even consider such proposals as those your brother would make.
Mary But you cannot mean to live there without making some improvements?
Edmund I mean to do as much as needs to be done, but certainly no more. So long as it is comfortable it will suit and I will be happy there.
Mary I have always believed that a large income is the best recipe for happiness, Mr Bertram.
Edmund Is that your ambition, Miss Crawford? To become very rich?
Mary To be sure. Is it not everyone's? Is it not yours?
Edmund I cannot intend anything which is beyond my power to command. My intentions are only not to be poor.
Mary Be poor and honest, by all means — but don't expect me to envy you. I have a greater respect for those that are rich and honest ——

Harkness enters

Harkness There was a moment's pause in which they both considered the gulf between their separate philosophies — and then Mary Crawford broke the mood:

Harkness exits

Mary Whatever your own ambition, Mr Bertram, I am sure that you would benefit from Henry's free advice. Remember how useful he was at Sotherton.

Henry, embarrassed by the subject, hurriedly concerns himself with the cards which Fanny is holding

Henry You must bid for another card, Miss Price. The queen will cost you eight.
Fanny Thank you, Mr Crawford.
Mary (*mischievously pursuing her theme*) We only spent a single day there and his genius took fire! We drove over in the morning, we came back in

the afternoon — but what was achieved in the short time that we were there does not bear mentioning, does it, brother?

Henry I cannot remember much concerning the afternoon at Sotherton. It was a hot day, we seemed to be going in all directions — it was hard to contemplate what one was about ... Let me see, Lady Bertram bids a dozen for that queen — no, no, it is not worth a dozen. She will let it pass.

Lady Bertram I will let it pass.

Henry (*to Fanny*) I would not wish to be judged by what took place at Sotherton. I am a changed man since then, Miss Price.

Mrs Norris William — when next you are granted shore-leave, you must hope that Mr and Mrs Rushworth are back in residence — for I am sure that they would make you welcome and Sotherton is a sight to see.

William I am sure it is, ma'am — and far too grand a place, from all that I have heard about it, to wish to welcome a scrubby midshipman through its doors.

Sir Thomas Nonsense, William. When you do meet Mr Rushworth, you will find him eager and willing to regard all of our family's connections as his own.

Mary (*looking over Edmund's shoulder*) No, no, Mr Bertram.

Edmund has been about to play a card, but Mary returns to his hand and plays another for him

Edmund Thank you.

William I am sure that I shall, sir. But I am not sure that I would feel worthy of that regard.

With which, William moves away from the card-tables and stands apart, lost in his own thoughts

Mrs Grant Are you enjoying Speculation, your ladyship?

Lady Bertram Very entertaining. Very odd. I don't know what it is all about. I am hardly to see my cards and Mr Crawford does everything for me. I do not lift a finger. I am enjoying it immensely.

Mrs Norris Sister, that is three tricks you have taken already. Sir Thomas, Lady Bertram has got three tricks already!

Sir Thomas Whatever it is that you are not doing, my dear, you appear to be doing it very well. I am beaten.

Sir Thomas lays down his cards. Fanny, at the other table, having noted William's downcast mood, makes a similar observation

Fanny I am out of this first game too.

Braithwaite enters

Braithwaite Henry, who had been advising both Fanny and Lady Bertram, looked at the cards that Fanny was holding and, puzzled, shook his head, advising her to play her hand. Fanny smiled, shook her head too, laying down her cards and crossed to join her brother as the game continued.

Fanny William? Are you unhappy?

William I was thinking — tonight is the Assembly Night in Portsmouth. If I was with the ship, I would have been at the dance.

Fanny Do you wish you were at Portsmouth, William?

William No, Fanny. I do not. Nor even at the Assembly Night Dance. I would not find a partner.

Lady Bertram What are trumps? Are they hearts or diamonds? I find the red cards quite confusing.

Henry Spades are trumps, your ladyship.

Lady Bertram Oh — spades.

William The girls in Portsmouth have little time for common midshipmen. Do you remember the Gregorys' girls?

Fanny We used to play with them. They were the best friends that we had.

William Not any longer. These days they will hardly speak to me. Lucy is being courted by a lieutenant.

Fanny You will get your commission, William. These things take time.

William Not time, Fanny. Influence.

Fanny But you will! You must look upon the waiting as one of those hardships that are a sailor's lot — like bad weather or — or having the long-boat sunk beneath you. But when you *are* a lieutenant, William — only think, when you are a lieutenant — we shall both of us feel so proud.

William I begin to think I shall never be a lieutenant, Fanny.

Fanny William, you must not say such things. You must not even think them. Our uncle never mentions your promotion, but I am sure that he will do everything that is within his power to see that you are granted it.

William Our uncle, Fanny, knows no-one at the Admiralty.

Braithwaite It occurred to them that Sir Thomas was possibly within earshot and so William changed the subject.

William Are you fond of dancing, Fanny?

Fanny Yes — very.

William Do you know what I would really enjoy? I would like to go to a ball with you and see you dance. I would dance with you, if you would dare to dance with me — for nobody here would know who I was — and I should like to partner you again. Do you remember when we used to dance together? When we were children in the street?

Fanny To the music played by that organ-grinder with the big moustache.

William And with a monkey, with a red-embroidered jacket and a matching hat, on a silver chain? You were much the better dancer than me, Fanny. I suppose that these days you are even better still?

Fanny (*shaking her head*) These days I rarely dance.

William False modesty is not a virtue, Fanny. (*Turning to Sir Thomas*) Is my sister a good dancer, sir? Does she put the rest to shame?

Sir Thomas William, I have never ever seen Fanny dance. But I am sure that she will acquit herself like a gentlewoman when you and I are granted that opportunity. What's more, I shall see you do have the indulgence before you leave Northamptonshire. (*He rises, moves to a prominent position in the room, clears his throat, loudly, drawing everyone's attention*) I have decided to hold a ball.

There is a general murmur of approval

Mrs Norris Oh, but you have my every approval, Sir Thomas. An excellent proposal. All that needs to be decided upon is a reason for the occasion. Ideally we should wait until dear Julia is home again and dearest Maria is in residence at Sotherton. A welcome home celebration for both of your dear, darling daughters.

Sir Thomas My daughters have their pleasures at Brighton, and I hope they are both happy. But the dance which I am contemplating will be for their cousins: William and Fanny. If Maria and Julia could both attend, our satisfaction would undoubtedly be more complete — but their absence will not debar the others of amusement.

Lady Bertram I shall look forward to it — provided I am not to be worn out on the occasion by all of the beforehand tiresome arranging. But you are so skilled in those matters, sister, I shall have no qualms in leaving everything to you ...

Henry draws Lady Bertram's attention as he lays down her hand of cards

Dear me! Have I won the game? And usually I have no head at all for card games.

Mrs Norris You have certainly had the beating of me. (*Rising*) Only look at the clock! Fanny, did you not think to remind us that we ordered the carriage to be outside exactly on the hour?

Fanny I forgot, Aunt Norris.

Mrs Norris You must not forget. You should always consider the coachman and the horses, Fanny. You should not bear to keep old Wilcox waiting.

Lady Bertram Where is my shawl? I must have my shawl.

Lady Bertram's shawl is over the back of her chair. Fanny drapes the shawl around Lady Bertram's shoulders

Dr Grant It is a pleasant evening. We should happily have strolled across the park.
Sir Thomas You shall do no such thing — so long as I have carriages and stables.
Mrs Norris We shall speed you on your way.

The Bertrams, Grants, Crawfords and Mrs Norris exit

William and Fanny gleefully hold each other's glance as the Lights fade and the card-tables and chairs are struck

William Only think of it, Fanny — a ball! And on our account.
Braithwaite He invited her into his arms and she accepted — and they performed a high-spirited jig around the room.

Braithwaite exits

William and Fanny dance

Scene 4

The Grounds, Mansfield Park

The night of the ball, which is being held outdoors. The occasion is enhanced by a chain of Japanese lanterns which have been strung from the branches of the trees. There is a garden bench, downstage, and possibly other similar benches on either side of the stage

As William and Fanny dance off in one direction, Harkness and Gipton enter

Gipton The ball is taking place this very night. Invitations have been despatched and, all across the county, young ladies have been going to their beds at night, their heads chock-a-block with happy cares — Fanny Price not least.
Harkness Mrs Norris, having entered into the spirit of the occasion — as much as she is capable of entering into the spirit of anything — decided that it shall be an alfresco entertainment ——
Gipton She has taken all of the organization upon herself.

In order to facilitate her quick-change into her ball gown, we hear Mrs Norris off stage

Mrs Norris (*off*) Harkness!
Harkness Yes, ma'am?

Mrs Norris (*off*) Not there, man! Lower! Lower!
Harkness (*looking up at the lanterns*) Lower! Lower!

The string of lanterns is lowered from off stage, and apparently to Mrs Norris's satisfaction

Braithwaite enters, followed by Sir Thomas and Lady Bertram who sit at either end of the downstage garden bench

Braithwaite While Lady Bertram has continued to sit in her usual place without being inconvenienced by the preparations.
Harkness Happily, occasioned partly by circumstance and partly by good fortune, the Bertram sons and daughters are all back at Mansfield Park in time for the celebration ——
Gipton But though it does his lordship's ageing heart a power of good to see his family reunited, his children's presence raises several questions of the heart and leaves several of them unanswered.

During the following, the characters enter as referred to, bow or curtsy their acknowledgement to Sir Thomas and Lady Bertram, and then move to one or other side of the stage

Braithwaite Tom Bertram, who loves manly things the most, like horse-racing and playing cards and heavy drinking, is back from London, bringing with him Mr Yates ——

Tom and Mr Yates enter

—who thinks himself in love with Julia Bertram.
Harkness Miss Julia though ——

Julia enters

—— can barely concern herself in passing the time of day with Mr Yates, having only just recovered from her own heartbreak at having lost Mr Rushworth ——

Mr Rushworth enters

—— to say nothing of his entire estate, to her only sister, Maria, now Mrs Rushworth.
Gipton While that young lady, Maria Bertram as was ——

Maria enters

— has now sufficient leisure time on her hands to remember that she married Mr Rushworth in haste in order to forget Henry Crawford, while her younger brother ——
Braithwaite — Edmund Bertram ——

Edmund enters

— still believes himself to be in love with Mary Crawford ——

Mary enters

— a young lady who might see her way to love him in return, if only he was in a position to afford her, while Miss Crawford's brother ——
Gipton — Henry Crawford ——

Henry enters

— whose firm intention it had been to have Fanny Price fall in love with him, now — and somewhat to his own surprise — is finding himself falling in love with Fanny Price.
Harkness Fanny Price, meanwhile ——

Fanny enters

— and being Fanny Price, has never ever since her childhood looked twice at any man excepting Edmund Bertram.

With most of the company now standing, in couples, around the park, Fanny, ravishing in a new ball gown, stands alone and apart, looking shyly around

Sir Thomas Fanny is looking extremely elegant.
Lady Bertram She looks very well. Duval helped her dress. I sent Duval to dress her.
Harkness Mrs Norris somewhat willingly decided to partially abandon mourning for the occasion.

Mrs Norris sweeps in grandly, wearing a black ball gown trimmed with gold. But she is not best pleased when Lady Bertram makes no mention of her finery

Sir Thomas stands

Lady Bertram Do you not think that Fanny looks a positive picture, sister? I let her have Duval to dress her.

Mrs Norris Fanny has every reason to look a positive picture, with all of her advantages — brought up in this family as she has been, and with all of the benefits of her cousins' manners before her.

William enters during the following, followed by Dr and Mrs Grant

Sir Thomas beckons Fanny across

Sir Thomas You are engaged for the first dance, Fanny?

Fanny No, sir.

Sir Thomas In which circumstance, Mr Crawford has kindly offered to accompany you.

Fanny It is most kind of Mr Crawford, sir. But as I have so little skill and even less experience in the ballroom — I was intending to leave the first dance to braver souls.

Sir Thomas My dear child, it is your ball. You must lead the first dance. It is expected of you.

Fanny Me, sir ... ?

Braithwaite Fanny glanced around and, to her horror, saw that all of the guests were looking in her direction.

Fanny But I cannot, sir! May it not be settled otherwise?

Sir Thomas No, it must be so, my dear.

Henry Miss Price? (*He offers Fanny his hand*) Follow me and together we will do well.

The music for the Minuet begins and Fanny, in some trepidation, allows Henry to lead her on to the floor. The other couples form up behind them, including William who partners Mrs Norris, and Dr Grant and Mrs Grant. Only Sir Thomas and Lady Bertram sit out the dance which continues during the following

Sir Thomas Who is that young man with Julia?

Lady Bertram He is Mr Yates.

Sir Thomas That theatrical fellow? I thought that we had bade our farewells to Mr Yates some weeks ago.

Lady Bertram So we had — and he is come back again with Tom.

Sir Thomas Then I rather wish that he had not.

As the Minuet continues, the dancers change partners and Fanny finds herself with Edmund. They may either continue the conversation as they dance, or move away from the others

Edmund Fanny, we must talk. You must save an entire dance for me.

Fanny Whichever one will please you, Edmund. I am entirely free.

Edmund So am I, alas. She has just told me that she will never dance with me again. Can you imagine that? What am I to do? Surely she cannot be serious? Can she be serious, do you think?

Fanny It is not for me to say, Edmund. I cannot know how Miss Crawford reasons.

By which point Fanny and Edmund will have stopped dancing, though the Minuet may continue behind them as they converse downstage

Edmund She has made her reasoning abundantly clear to me. She has never danced with a clergyman before, or so she says, and she never will again.

Fanny I am sorry that something has occurred that distresses you, Edmund. This should be an evening entirely of pleasure. My uncle meant it so.

Edmund Yes, yes — and I am sure it will be, Fanny. It will end all right, I'm sure. As I am leaving home tomorrow ——

Fanny Leaving? To go where? You had not told me.

Edmund To go to Hertfordshire. To stay with an old friend. Mr Owen. You must have heard me mention him?

Fanny I may have done. Shall you be away long?

Edmund A month, perhaps — perhaps two ... Fanny, about Miss Crawford ——

Fanny If you wish to discuss Miss Crawford with me, Edmund, I am willing to listen. But you must not ask my advice. I am not competent on that subject.

Edmund You are right, Fanny. And I do not seek advice. I only wanted to talk to you.

Fanny You must not say anything about that lady that you might later regret. The time may come, Edmund, when Miss Crawford and yourself ——

Edmund Dearest Fanny, the chances of that seem to grow less and less — and even if it should, I have never said one word to you — nor would I ever — that is detrimental to Miss Crawford ——

Fanny Edmund! She will hear you!

Miss Crawford is approaching them, accompanied by William with whom she has been dancing

Miss Crawford.

Mary Miss Price — you have a most persistent brother. I have promised him one dance already, and he has almost succeeded in convincing me that I should grant him another later in the evening. Mr Bertram.

Edmund Miss Crawford.

Mary Were you aware that your cousin is leaving Mansfield Park tomorrow?

Fanny To stay with an old friend, Mr Owen. Edmund had told me, yes.

Mary And he will have told you also, no doubt, that Mr Owen has three grown sisters, none of them married? I see that you were not aware of the fact. Well, I do not think that we should question him about them further. I am sure, without having to ask, that they are all three very accomplished and very pleasing — and that one of them is very pretty.

Fanny How do you know?

Mary There is a beauty in every family. It is a regular thing. You were also asking for a second dance, Mr Bertram? Perhaps I should reconsider, in the hope that I shall not be entirely forgotten when you are surrounded by the trio of Miss Owens. I shall consult my card again — if you will accompany me until this dance is finished, I have put it down somewhere — possibly in the conservatory.

Mary and Edmund take up the dance again

William There is something that I must tell you, Fanny.

Fanny If it is something you think I would not wish to know, William, I would rather you kept it until morning.

William Tomorrow will be too late, Fanny. I will not be here tomorrow. That is what I have to tell you — I am leaving in the morning.

Fanny But I thought that you could stay for two more days, at least?

William Mr Crawford is taking a coach to London in the morning. He has suggested I accompany him. It will save both time and expense — it would be foolish to turn down his generosity.

Fanny Yes, of course. Edmund is leaving and now you are leaving. Less than an hour ago, I was looking forward to this evening.

William But you shall enjoy this evening, Fanny. We must both of us enjoy ourselves. It is *our* ball.

The Minuet has begun again and, again, Henry invites Fanny to partner him. Sir Thomas and Lady Bertram are still watching from the downstage garden bench

Sir Thomas Fanny dances very well.

Lady Bertram Looking back, Sir Thomas, I am so glad that we took her into our family as we did. For now the others are grown up we feel the benefit.

Sir Thomas She has been a good companion for you, my dear.

Lady Bertram And still is. Now that our own are all grown up and going off: Maria is Mrs Rushworth; Tom seems to spend more time in travelling than he spends at home; Edmund will soon be taking up his living; there is only Julia — and when Julia is gone, we shall have Fanny to depend upon.

Sir Thomas I am proud of her. She deserves everything she has become.

Lady Bertram Yes, and it is a comfort to think that, whatever else may happen, we shall always have Fanny. She will never leave us.

Sir Thomas and Lady Bertram exit as the dance ends. The other dancers have already drifted off, to seek refreshment or to walk around the grounds, only Fanny and Henry remain

Fanny My brother tells me, Mr Crawford, that he is journeying to London with you in the morning?

Henry I was pleased to be able to offer him that courtesy.

Fanny It came as some surprise to me. I had not known that you were planning such a visit?

Henry A business matter has arisen, Miss Price, which demands my immediate attention.

Fanny Fortuitously, Mr Crawford — for it has saved William both expense and inconvenience.

Henry I cannot believe that anything that deprives me of such loveliness as yours, Miss Price, could ever be deemed fortuitous.

Fanny Mr Crawford! You must not! Should not!

Henry Must not? Should not? Tomorrow's leave-taking is much too close for me to hold back now from honest truth. Forgive me, Fanny, but you are all loveliness tonight ...

Fanny (*embarrassed*) Good-night, Mr Crawford.

Fanny exits and Mary enters

The dialogue begins and we realize that we have 'jumped forward' some several minutes in time

Mary *Marry* her! You're going to marry Fanny Price?

Henry She was beautiful tonight. She is gentle. She is kind. I am fairly caught. I don't know why you should be so surprised.

Mary Nor I. I think it is quite wonderful news, Henry. That after all your wanderings, and dalliances, and heart-breakings, you should have found your fate in Mansfield. Fanny Price!

Henry And what of your fate, Mary? Is that also to be settled in Mansfield?

Mary I think I could love Edmund Bertram, Henry, and with all my heart. I think I am in love with him now. But I would not — could not — love being a country parson's wife. Oh, but you could not have chosen better. There is not a better girl in the world. She has no money, of course, but then

you do not want for fortune. Her connections could not be improved upon
— the Bertrams are among the first people in the county. But go on, go on!

Henry Go on with what?

Mary Tell me more. What are your plans? Does she know of her own
happiness? Did you ask her tonight?

Henry No. Not yet.

Mary Why not? You should have whispered at her in the moonlight, Henry,
while you were dancing.

Henry I shall wait until after I am back from London. She will not refuse me,
do you think?

Mary You? How could she? You have said yourself, the poor child is too
gentle and good-hearted to refuse anything to anyone. No, that is not true.
I cannot believe that little Fanny would marry without love — but she will
not be able to stop herself from loving you.

Henry And I cannot stop myself from matrimony.

Mary Henry, my best congratulations. Do you know, brother, what I can't
help thinking about?

Henry Tell me, sister?

Mary All those Christmases we might be spending at Mansfield Park.

Henry All those card games.

Mary All that mulled wine.

Henry And all those amateur theatricals when Sir Thomas is in Antigua.

Mary "Only a woman can teach the science of herself."

Henry "Doubt that the stars are fire,
Doubt that the earth doth move,
Doubt truth to be a liar,
But never doubt — I love!"

*As Henry and Mary exit, the Lights dim and come up instantly for the next
scene*

SCENE 5

The Drawing-Room, Mansfield Park

An angry Sir Thomas confronts a distraught Fanny Price

Sir Thomas Refuse him?

Fanny Yes, sir.

Sir Thomas This is very strange! There is something in this which is beyond
my comprehension. Am I to understand that you mean to refuse Henry
Crawford?

Fanny Yes, sir.
Sir Thomas Refuse Henry Crawford?
Fanny Yes, sir.
Sir Thomas Upon what plea? For what reason?
Fanny I — I cannot like him, sir, well enough to marry him.

Gipton enters

Gipton Sir Thomas found himself confronted with a conundrum. His nineteen-year-old niece was prepared to spurn the security and prosperity of an excellent marriage to Henry Crawford for reasons such as he could not comprehend. He had come to love Fanny Price like a daughter — but he could not love a rebellious spirit such as either of his own daughters ever dared have. He did not believe that any daughter could behave like this.
Sir Thomas Here is a young man wishing to pay his addresses to you, with everything to recommend him: not merely situation in life, fortune and character, but with more than common agreeableness, with address and conversation pleasing to everybody.
Fanny Yes, sir.
Sir Thomas You are aware of what he has been able to do for your own brother?
Fanny Yes, sir. He has been most kind. He has managed to secure William his promotion.
Sir Thomas I could not have done it for him. Mr Crawford has been to London. He has a relative high-up at the Admiralty. Entirely due to Mr Crawford's representation, Fanny, your brother William is now a serving lieutenant in His Majesty's fleet.
Fanny And I am infinitely grateful to Mr Crawford, sir. But I cannot marry him.
Sir Thomas I am half inclined to the opinion, Fanny, that you do not quite know your own feelings.
Fanny Oh, yes, sir! Indeed I do!
Sir Thomas You must have been aware of a particularity in Mr Crawford's manner to you? You must have noticed his attentions? I had, certainly, and never perceived them to be unpleasant to you.
Fanny His attentions were always ... what I did not like.
Sir Thomas This is beyond me. This requires explanation. Young as you are and, so far as I am aware, having the acquaintanceship of so few young gentlemen, I am beginning to wonder whether ... ?

Fanny, deeply embarrassed, lowers her face, shakes her head

Fanny (*in a voice not much above a whisper*) There is no-one else, sir.

Sir Thomas I am an advocate for early marriage and would have every young man, with sufficient income, settled as soon as possible. My eldest son, your cousin, Mr Bertram, has shown no signs as yet in that direction. His brother, Edmund, I sometimes think, because of his nature and his calling, is much more likely to marry early than his brother. Indeed, I have begun to wonder lately whether he might have found the woman he could love — a lady not too far removed from Mr Crawford. Have you thought that too?

Fanny (*close to tears*) Yes, sir. I believe that to be true.

Sir Thomas You are not my daughter. You do not owe me the duty of a child of mine. But if you can examine your own heart, Fanny, and find that it acquits you of ingratitude ——

Fanny (*unable to hold back her tears any longer*) I am sorry. I am very sorry. I am very sorry indeed.

Sir Thomas Sorry! Yes, I hope you are sorry. But there is no use in all of those tears. (*He gives her his handkerchief*) Dry them up, child. It is not only to me that you should be making these apologies. It is to Mr Crawford.

Fanny He is not in the house?

Sir Thomas He arrived here early and I had breakfast with him. He is in my room and waiting to talk to you.

Fanny But there is nothing further that I have to say to him. I made my intention clear, I hope, when we spoke yesterday.

Sir Thomas You made nothing clear to him, miss — or why else would he have come round this morning and raised the matter with me? All that he requests is five minutes of your time — and you must give him a plain straightforward "No" yourself and put an end to it.

Fanny No, Uncle! I cannot face him again! I will not go to him. Tell him! Tell him that I will not see him!

Sir Thomas I shall see him. I shall tell him where you are to be found. I cannot force you to go to him, Fanny — equally, if Mr Crawford wishes to come to you to convince you of his feelings, I cannot deny him that right either.

Sir Thomas goes out. Braithwaite enters

Braithwaite Fanny sobbed to herself, quietly, and stared fearfully at the door — and waited. There was a knock. She held both her silence and her breath. There was another knock and then Edmund entered. She was overjoyed.

Fanny Edmund, you are home!

Edmund There are some legal matters to be attended to regarding Thornton Lacey. It was fortunate, it seems, that I chose to come back early.

Fanny Have you seen your father? Did you know that Mr Crawford is in the house?

Edmund I have not spoken with Sir Thomas, no — but I have seen Mr Crawford. I have just left him.

Fanny Did he tell you that he wishes to marry me? I have told my uncle that I cannot marry Mr Crawford but he has called me ungrateful. I should not marry him, should I, Edmund?

Edmund In what you have done so far, you have been right, Fanny ——

Fanny You cannot know how pleased I am that you are here, Edmund.

Edmund — but you must agree to see Henry Crawford.

Fanny No, Edmund.

Edmund Fanny, he must be allowed to pursue his suit with you.

Fanny is shaking her head, slowly but firmly

You must, Fanny. Believe me, if you will only grant him the time that he deserves, then both his feelings and your own will be granted their rewards.

Fanny We are opposites, Edmund, Mr Crawford and myself. We do not have one single taste in common.

Edmund So much the better. He is lively; you are serious. His spirits will embolden yours.

Fanny We should make each other miserable.

Edmund You are mistaken, Fanny, you do have tastes in common.

Fanny We have nothing in common, Edmund. Nothing — nothing. I do not even like Mr Crawford. I did not like him at the time of *Lovers' Vows*. I did not like the way that he went out of his way to hurt Mr Rushworth. I did not like the attentions that he paid at Sotherton to Maria.

Edmund What happened during *Lovers' Vows* is in the past, Fanny. And if Henry Crawford behaved badly, then so did my sister. But we were all wrong together.

Fanny Oh, Edmund, you were not to blame.

Edmund You have been happy here at Mansfield Park and it will be hard for you to leave. I only wish that Mr Crawford knew you as well as I do — for between us, I think, we would know how to win you.

Fanny I will never marry Mr Crawford.

Edmund But it would be right for you to do so. If you were to marry him it would unite our families. My parents would be sure to be pleased and I know that it would delight Miss Crawford ——

Fanny Miss Crawford! Miss Crawford! My uncle tells me that I should marry Henry Crawford for the sake of my parents and my brothers and sisters. You say that I should marry him to please Mary Crawford! You are wrong to say that I would find it hard to leave Mansfield Park. Leaving Mansfield Park may prove to be the easiest thing that I have ever had to do!

Fanny rushes from the room, as the Lights darken for the next scene

Edmund exits

SCENE 6

The Drive, Mansfield Park

It is night. The scene is played downstage in a small pool of light cast by a lantern which is held aloft by Harkness

Gipton enters, carrying a heavy trunk

Gipton Miss Fanny may not have found it difficult to avoid meeting Henry Crawford that day, or to depart Mansfield Park — but packing the boxes she had decided to take with her was enough to keep me busy for most of a morning and the best part of an afternoon.

Harkness Leave them there, girl. I'll see them safely on board the coach.

Gipton There's more to come.

Harkness Fanny Price decided that, for the first time since she had been with the Bertrams, she would go back and stay with her family in Portsmouth. Sir Thomas was in favour of the visit, reasoning that a brief return to the frugalities and shortcomings of Portsmouth might make his niece all the more appreciative of the elegances and luxuries of Mansfield Park. In addition to which, his lordship reasoned, her time away from Henry Crawford might prove a case of absence making the heart grow fonder ——

Gipton But if Miss Fanny left for Portsmouth with more luggage than seemed necessary, before many weeks had passed, Miss Julia took her leave too, with far less luggage and at a later hour than might have been deemed appropriate——

Mr Yates enters

Mr Yates Julia! Julia!

At Mr Yates's approach, Harkness hands the lantern to Gipton, picks up the trunk and they exit, hastily

Julia, are you there?

Julia enters, carrying a small case

Julia Mr Yates? Is that you?

They locate each other in the dark and embrace

Mr Yates Is that all you are taking with you?
Julia It is all that there was time to bring.
Mr Yates This way. Through the trees. I have a carriage waiting in the road
  beyond the park.
Julia Where are we going?
Mr Yates Inverness.
Julia Inverness?
Mr Yates Yes.
Julia Heavens!

*Mr Yates puts an arm round Julia's shoulder and leads her off as Gipton
enters, in a spot*

Gipton And, as if having one daughter elope into the night was not enough
  for any gentleman to bear, before a month was gone there was much worse
  news to be faced ...

Gipton exits

The Lights come up on the next Scene

Scene 7

The Drawing-Room, Mansfield Park

*Sir Thomas, newspaper in hand, Lady Bertram and Mrs Norris are frozen in
stunned silence*

Harkness enters

Harkness Mr Rushworth is here, Sir Thomas ——

*But Mr Rushworth, looking flustered, has already bustled into the room
and Harkness withdraws discreetly*

Sir Thomas It is true then?
Mr Rushworth You have heard?

*Sir Thomas holds up his newspaper to indicate the source of his information
and Mr Rushworth is even further distressed*

It has been printed in the newspaper?

Sir Thomas Today. So it is true?

Mrs Norris We were hoping against hope that it might have been printed in error — or, by some happy circumstance, it was not you, or ——

Lady Bertram That she could so much as contemplate such a deed!

Sir Thomas And it is Henry Crawford with whom Mrs Rushworth has absconded?

Mr Rushworth It does not mention him by name? (*A glimmer of hope*) Perhaps they have not set down my name either? Or Maria's?

Mrs Norris They have not identified anyone by their full names, Mr Rushworth. They are obliged not to do so.

Mr Rushworth Heaven be praised for that!

Sir Thomas Save your praises to heaven, Mr Rushworth, and settle for condemnation of the editor. There is little left to the imagination, alas. Read it for yourself.

Mr Rushworth I dare not look.

Sir Thomas It will not improve. Better to do it now and get it over with.

Harkness enters

Harkness Mr Rushworth took the newspaper in some trepidation. He glanced nervously at all three of them in turn and was about to force himself to read the offending paragraph when ——

Edmund enters

— Mr Rushworth was more than grateful for this temporary reprieve.

Mr Rushworth Mr Bertram! This is an wholly unexpected pleasure! I had thought that you would have been at Thornton Lacey? (*Suddenly aghast*) The news of my misfortune has not been spread around Thornton Lacey already? It is not because of this that you are back at Mansfield Park?

Lady Bertram My eldest son has been stricken ill, Mr Rushworth. He is confined to bed. Edmund has come home to nurse his brother.

Mr Rushworth Not seriously ill, I trust?

Sir Thomas He will recover. It is commendable of you, Mr Rushworth, to place my family's problems before your own — but don't you think that you should make yourself aware of the contents of that newspaper?

Mr Rushworth Yes! Yes! (*He locates the relevant passage. After much throat clearing, reading*) "It is with infinite concern that this journal seeks to announce to the world a matrimonial fracas in the family of Mr 'R' of Wimpole Street." That is me of a certainty! The whole of England will recognize me by that description. 'R' for Rushworth and I own a house in Wimpole Street. I am pin-pointed with deadly accuracy. Even though there was no fracas in Wimpole Street. That information is entirely false. I was in Bath, visiting my mother who chanced to be visiting. My wife was staying with friends of ours in Twickenham. I call them "friends" — I used to think them friends — they were no friends of mine, apparently. Henry Crawford had constant access to that house, in my absence, or so it has since transpired. Why does this state that there was a fracas in Wimpole Street?

Sir Thomas shrugs and Lady Bertram and Mrs Norris shake their heads as Mr Rushworth continues

"Mr 'R' of Wimpole Street; the beautiful Mrs 'R' who had promised to become a leader in the fashionable world, having quitted her husband's roof in company with the well-known and captivating Mr 'C' ——" Well-known and captivating! That is Henry Crawford. He captivated Maria, certainly. "— the intimate friend and associate of Mr 'R'." Well, they have that wrong too. He was never an intimate friend of mine and he is no longer an associate. There is more that is wrong about this article than there is right — but is that not generally the way with newspapers? "— It is not known, even to the editor of this journal, whither they are gone." There is one thing right. Maria is beautiful. How am I to manage without her?

Lady Bertram When did this happen?

Sir Thomas When did she go off with the scoundrel?

Lady Bertram Did you attempt to follow them?

Mr Rushworth I have no idea whither they are gone myself. It is something I have in common with this journal's editor. (*Handing the newspaper back to Sir Thomas*) Thank you.

Sir Thomas It is a disgraceful and entirely unnecessary piece of journalism — but then, this whole business is disgraceful.

Mr Rushworth If you will excuse me. I am on my way to Sotherton. I would hope to attend my mother before she too is informed of it from another source.

Edmund I will walk with you to your coach.

Lady Bertram Mr Rushworth?

Mr Rushworth Lady Bertram?

Lady Bertram Will you take her back?

Mr Rushworth (*after a pause*) She will not come back, ma'am. He has always held this fascination for Mrs Rushworth. (*To Edmund*) You may remember the afternoon at Sotherton Court? And then there was the business of the — (*breaking down at last*) of the — the play-acting ...

Mr Rushworth hurries from the room to cover his embarrassment, accompanied by Edmund

Sir Thomas A thoroughly disgraceful business. Sister-in-law?

Mrs Norris Yes, Sir Thomas?

Sir Thomas Without wishing to apportion blame, there were things that were encouraged in my absence that should not have been encouraged.

Mrs Norris (*bowing her head*) Yes, Sir Thomas.

Sir Thomas And to think I stood here in this very room and castigated Fanny for disapproving of the scoundrel.

Lady Bertram Sir Thomas?

Sir Thomas Yes, ma'am?

Lady Bertram Would you be so kind as to summon me a servant?

Sir Thomas Maria?

Lady Bertram Thomas?

Sir Thomas Has it ever so much as crossed your mind to cross a room and summon a servant for yourself?

Lady Bertram (*genuinely puzzled*) No, Thomas. Why should it?

Sir Thomas No matter.

Sir Thomas exits as Harkness enters from another direction

Harkness Some things don't change at Mansfield Park ... You rang, mi-lady?

Lady Bertram Pug needs his exercise.

Harkness (*taking the dog*) Yes, your ladyship. The lap-dog still requires regular attention. Carried about from silken cushion to silver supper-bowl — and they refer to it as "a dog's life".

Harkness exits and Braithwaite enters. During the following, Gipton enters and the Lights fade to a spot

Braithwaite Mrs Norris resolved to quit Mansfield Park.

Mrs Norris exits

Sir Thomas's opinion of her had been sinking from the day of his return from Antigua. Her going proved such a relief that, had she not left bitter remembrances behind her, there might have been danger of his learning almost to approve the evil which produced such a good.

Gipton (*in a spot*) And there was better news of Tom. He was well enough to get up and be taken down into the drawing-room where Edmund would read to him.

Gipton exits

The Lights come up on Tom, well-wrapped up against the draughty night-

air and sitting in a bath-chair, as Edmund reads the concluding paragraph of The Vicar of Wakefield

Edmund "My family was assembled by the cheerful fireside. My two little ones sat upon each knee, the rest of the company by their partners. I had nothing now on this side of the grave to wish for: all my cares were over, my pleasure was unspeakable. It now only remained that my gratitude in good fortune should exceed my former submission in adversity. (*He closes the book*)

Gipton enters during the following

Tom Is that the end?
Edmund It is, Tom, yes.
Tom It's very good.
Edmund But as one volume is put down another one may be picked up. Tomorrow, if you are feeling well enough, we shall begin another book.
Gipton (*bobbing at Edmund*) Begging your pardon, Mr Edmund.
Edmund Yes, Gipton?
Gipton May I trundle Mr Bertram back to the dining-room? His dinner-time broth is hotted up.
Tom (*grimacing*) Oh, God.

Braithwaite enters

Braithwaite The hotted broth was meant as a punishment, not cure. Strong drink had brought about his downfall and now he was denied it. He had been carousing at Newmarket with some friends and falling down, then being left there lying outdoors all night.
Gipton Still, there are some small signs of slight improvement — which is more than can be said for either of the Bertram daughters.

Gipton pushes Tom off

Braithwaite As for Mr Edmund, his future lot in life would seem to be that of a lonely parish priest. So much for the Bertram children — a case of all's ill that ends ill ... ?

Fanny enters, dressed for travelling

Fanny Edmund.
Edmund Fanny!
Fanny You look well.

Edmund I thought you were lost to us in Portsmouth.

Fanny I had a letter from your father, requesting my return. I thought you were in Thornton Lacey — and married, possibly to Miss Crawford.

Edmund We quarrelled, Fanny, over her brother's behaviour. Can you imagine? She saw nothing wrong in what went on between Henry Crawford and my sister. Their crime, according to Miss Crawford, was not in conducting their clandestine affair — they suffered, Miss Crawford told me in as many words, only from a lack of discretion.

Fanny And what did you say to her in return?

Edmund Nothing — nothing that she seemed to comprehend. This is what the world has done to her — a woman whom nature has so richly endowed. She is spoilt, Fanny, spoilt.

Fanny And so you have been sitting about, have you, since she left? Suffering disappointment and regret, grieving over what was, and wishing for what never could be?

Edmund I have not only sat grieving over the past, Fanny. I have given some thought to the future.

Fanny The future?

Edmund Yes. I have not stopped thinking about you.

Fanny What about me?

Edmund About you and me. About Edmund Bertram and Fanny Price.

Fanny If you will excuse me, Edmund. I have unpacking to attend to. (*She turns her back on him and moves to exit*)

Edmund Fanny!

Fanny pauses, but does not turn

Miss Crawford always spoke well of you. "Henry has thrown away," she said, after you had gone, "such a woman as he will ever see again. She would have made him happy for ever." If you would wish me to say more, Fanny, you must turn and look at me.

Fanny turns and stares at him accusingly

Fanny You do not deserve me, Edmund Bertram. I am much too good for you.

Edmund At least allow me opportunity.

Fanny How can you expect me to care for you when you have not ceased to care for Mary Crawford. And you have not ceased to care for her, have you? Have you? Answer me!

Edmund shrugs, hopelessly, unable to deny the charge. They face each other across the room, but they might be miles apart. Fanny is too hurt to seek his eyes while Edmund, in return, is too embarrassed to look at her

Harkness enters slowly

As Harkness speaks, Fanny and Edmund take tentative steps towards each other, finally standing close but without touching

Harkness I purposely abstain from dates, in order that every one of you may be at liberty to fix your own, aware that the cure of unconquerable passions, and the transfer of unchanging attachments, must vary as to time in different people — I only entreat you all to believe that, exactly at the time when it was quite natural, Edmund Bertram did cease to care about Mary Crawford, and became as anxious to marry Fanny, as Fanny herself could desire.

Edmund Shall we be happy, Fanny, do you think?

Fanny With so much true merit, Edmund, and so much true love, and no want of friendship or of fortune, our happiness shall be as secure as earthly happiness can ever be.

Edmund takes Fanny in his arms

Harkness And so Fanny Price became Mrs Edmund Bertram, a country parson's wife — which was no more nor less than she had ever asked for.

Edmund kisses Fanny

Fanny Or, indeed, had ever wanted.

CURTAIN

FURNITURE AND PROPERTY LIST

ACT I
SCENE 1

On stage: *Chaise-longue. On it*: cushion
Small table. *On it*: small handbell
Chairs

Off stage: Small trunk (**Gipton**)
Cake stand containing cakes (**Braithwaite**)

Personal: **Lady Bertram**: imitation pug dog (used throughout)

SCENE 2

On stage: Blackboard and easel
Small school chair

Off stage: Writing box containing paper, ink, pens (**Edmund**)

SCENE 3

On stage: Garden seat

Off stage: Straw hat, small portable medicine chest (**Gipton**)
Small sea-going trunk (**Harkness**)

Personal: **Mourners**: black umbrellas

SCENE 4

On stage: Small tables
Chairs

Off stage: Tray of punch (**Braithwaite**)

Scene 5

On stage: Nil

Off stage: Large trunk (**Harkness**)

Scene 6

On stage: Decorative iron fence with gate
              2 garden benches

Off stage: Basket of vegetables, 2 wrapped cheeses and small basket of
              pheasant's eggs (**Mrs Norris**)

Personal: **Edmund**: watch

Scene 7

On stage: *Chaise-longue. On it*: cushion
              Small table. *On it*: small handbell
              Chairs

Off stage: Rostra, supports, curtains, benches and trunk containing props
              including a hat (**Tom, Mr Yates, Harkness, Stage Manage-
              ment**)
              Sewing-box (**Gipton**)
              Cake stand containing cakes (**Braithwaite**)
              Book (**Fanny**)
              Hat, ostrich feather, needle and thread (**Gipton**)
              Toolbox (**Carpenter**)

Personal: **Edmund**: playbook
              Mrs Grant: playbook
              Mary: playbook

ACT II
Scene 1

On stage: *Chaise-longue. On it*: cushion
Small table. *On it*: small handbell
Chairs
Small stack of books c

Off stage: Bridal gown (**Gipton**)
Bridegroom's wedding suit (**Harkness**)
Book, glass of wine (**Fanny**)

Personal: **Lady Bertram**: playbook
Tom: playbook
Edmund: playbook

Scene 2

On stage: Nil

Off stage: Letter (**Gipton**)
Copy of *The Times* (**Harkness**)
Seaman's chest (**Harkness**)

Scene 3

On stage: 2 green baize-covered tables
8 chairs. *On one*: **Lady Bertram**'s shawl

Off stage: Tray containing playing cards, pencils, paper (**Gipton**)

Scene 4

On stage: Garden bench downstage
Trees

SCENE 5

On stage: *Chaise-longue. On it*: cushion
              Small table. *On it*: small handbell
              Chairs

Personal: **Sir Thomas**: handkerchief

SCENE 7

On stage: *Chaise-longue. On it*: cushion
              Small table. *On it*: small handbell
              Chairs
              Newspaper for **Sir Thomas**

Off stage: Bath chair (**Tom**)
              Copy of *The Vicar of Wakefield* (**Edmund**)

LIGHTING PLOT

Property fittings required: chandelier for Act I, Scene 4.

Practical fittings required: string of Japanese lanterns for Act II, Scene 4.

Various interior and exterior settings.

To open: General lighting on drawing-room area

Cue 1	**Mrs Norris**: " ... our poor sister tomorrow." *Crossfade to spot on* **Harkness**	(Page 3)
Cue 2	**Harkness**: " ... of being first to welcome her." *Crossfade to separate area*	(Page 4)
Cue 3	**Mrs Norris** and **Fanny** exit *Crossfade to drawing-room area*	(Page 4)
Cue 4	**Gipton**: " ... for such a scrap of a girl ——" *Crossfade to the schoolroom*	(Page 6)
Cue 5	**Braithwaite**: " ... her aunt walked into the room." *Crossfade to dull lighting on downstage area*	(Page 8)
Cue 6	**Mourners**: "Amen." *Bring up full exterior sunshine effect*	(Page 9)
Cue 7	**Harkness**: "Hooked, gaffed and safely landed." *Crossfade to general interior effect on ballroom area with optional moonlight on upstage terrace area*	(Page 12)
Cue 8	**Gipton**: " ... pride of place beside him." *Crossfade to downstage area*	(Page 18)
Cue 9	**Harkness** exits *Crossfade to spot on* **Braithwaite**	(Page 20)

Cue 10 **Braithwaite:** " ... walk and admire ..." (Page 20)
Crossfade to exterior shaded effect on Wilderness area

Cue 11 **Mrs Norris** and **Fanny** exit (Page 29)
Fade to spots on **Harkness, Gipton** *and* **Braithwaite**

Cue 12 **Gipton:** " ... in thirteen weeks ..." (Page 29)
Crossfade to general interior lighting c

Cue 13 As the song ends (Page 32)
*Fade to black-out. When ready bring up general
   interior lighting*

Cue 14 **Edmund** hastens after **Fanny** (Page 37)
Fade to spot on **Braithwaite**

Cue 15 **Braithwaite:** " ... in order to learn their lines ..." (Page 37)
Bring up general interior lighting

Cue 16 **Edmund** exits (Page 38)
Fade to spot on **Fanny,** *bring up spot on* **Gipton**

Cue 17 **Harkness:** " ... Miss Crawford's doing." (Page 39)
Spot on **Braithwaite**

Cue 18 **Gipton:** "It was all misery now ——" (Page 39)
Crossfade to general interior lighting

ACT II

To open: Full lighting on drawing-room area

Cue 19 **Sir Thomas** and **Maria** exit (Page 54)
Fade lighting then return to previous level

Cue 20 **Harkness:** " ... the wedding ceremony." (Page 55)
Fade lighting then return to previous level

Cue 21 **Fanny** hastens off (Page 56)
Fade to spot on **Gipton**

Cue 22 **Gipton** exits. **Harkness** enters (Page 57)
Crossfade to spot on **Harkness**

Cue 23   **Harkness:** "The bride was elegantly dressed."   (Page 57)
            Fade up chapel interior lighting

Cue 24   **Henry** exits   (Page 59)
            Fade to spot on **Gipton**

Cue 25   **Gipton:** "Miss Price! Miss Price!"   (Page 59)
            Bring up full general lighting

Cue 26   **Fanny, William** and **Henry** exit   (Page 60)
            Fade to two spots on **Servants**

Cue 27   **Braithwaite:** " ... favour with Fanny Price."   (Page 60)
            Bring up full general lighting on drawing-room area

Cue 28   **William:** "Only think of it ..."   (Page 67)
            *Fade to exterior night effect; when ready bring up
                practicals, with covering light*

Cue 29   **Henry** and **Mary** exit   (Page 74)
            *Snap off practicals, dim lighting; bring up full
                lighting on drawing-room*

Cue 30   **Fanny** rushes from the room   (Page 77)
            Fade to covering spot for lantern downstage

Cue 31   **Gipton** and **Harkness** exit   (Page 78)
            Dim covering spot to minimum

Cue 32   **Gipton** enters   (Page 79)
            Crossfade to spot on **Gipton**

Cue 33   **Gipton** exits   (Page 79)
            Crossfade to full lighting on drawing-room area

Cue 34   **Braithwaite:** " ... which produced such a good." (Page 82)
            Fade to spot on **Gipton**

Cue 35   **Gipton** exits   (Page 83)
            Crossfade to full lighting on drawing-room area

EFFECTS PLOT

ACT I

Cue 1   To open Scene 4   (Page 12)
Country dance music, continue throughout scene

ACT II

Cue 2   **Henry:** " ... we will do well."   (Page 70)
Minuet music; continue throughout scene

Thou art gone from my gaze

Thomas Linley

Thou art gone from my gaze like a beau-ti-ful dream and I seek thee in vain by the mea-dow and stream; Oft I breathe thy dear name to the winds float-ing by but thy sweet voice is mute to my bo-som's lone sigh. In the still-ness of

The merry month of may

Minuet